NUMBER POWER™

A Cooperative Approach to Mathematics
and Social Development

Grade 3, Volume 1: Place Value, Mental
Computation, and Data
Analysis

Laurel Robertson

Shaila Regan

Marji Freeman

Julie Wellington Contestable

DEVELOPMENTAL STUDIES CENTER
2000 Embarcadero, Suite 305
Oakland, CA 94606

This material is based upon work supported by the National Science Foundation under Grant No. ESI-9150104.

Any opinions, findings, and conclusions, or recommendations expressed in this material are those of the author(s) and do not necessarily reflect the views of the National Science Foundation.

Number Power™ was developed by the Cooperative Mathematics Project, a program of the Developmental Studies Center, 2000 Embarcadero, Suite 305, Oakland, California 94606.

Design: Don Taka
Illustrations: Duane Bibby
Cover Design: John Sullivan/Visual Stategies

ISBN 1-57621-200-9

Contents

Acknowledgments

Many people were involved in the development and production of *Number Power*. We are grateful for their time, valuable suggestions, and encouragement.

In particular, we wish to express our deep appreciation to the Stuart Foundations of San Francisco and to Ted Lobman, president, for their faith in and support of our program.

We extend our sincere thanks to the Walter S. Johnson Foundation and staff, who provided not only encouragement, but also a bridging grant at a critical time.

We also wish to thank the members of our Advisory Board, who contributed enormously to the development of the *Number Power* program:

Joan Akers, California State Department of Education

Carne Barnett, Far West Laboratory for Educational Research and Development

Neil Davidson, University of Maryland

Carol Langbort, San Francisco State University

Nell Noddings, Stanford University

Ruth Parker, Collaborative Learning Associates, Ferndale, Washington

Paul Trafton, University of Northern Iowa

Jean Stenmark, EQUALS, Lawrence Hall of Science, University of California, Berkeley

Julian Weissglass, University of California, Santa Barbara

Many teachers piloted lessons and units, allowed us in their classrooms to teach or to observe, and provided us with feedback that helped shape the format and content of the program. We particularly wish to acknowledge the following teachers and math specialists:

California

Alameda City Unified School District
Jane Baldi

Albany City Unified School District
Nancy Johnson
Violet Nicholas
Susie Ronfeldt

Berkeley Unified School District
Carolyn Adams
Mary Ough

Moreland Elementary School District
Terry Baker
Pat Brigham
Wanda Binford
Cristine Bryant
Carolyn Cassell
Shari Clare
Jan Frosberg
Vivian Karpel
Lew Osborn
Terry Pomposo
Linda Stumpf
Gaby Tennant

Oakland Unified School District
Mike Butzen
Roz Haberkern
Alicia Rivera
Kathy Selleck
Ted Sugarman
Sue Tierney

Redwood City Elementary School District
Kris Dalrymple
Lisa Erskine
Frances Nuss
Ann Marie Sulzbach

Ross Elementary School District
Allison Quoyeser

John Swett Unified School District
Kay Balandra
Louise Bevilaqua
Alice Dorman
Marilyn Griego
Anita Pister
Jackie Schlemmer
Carol Westrich

San Ramon Valley Unified School District
Cindy Collins
Cheryl Gonzales
Deneka Horaleck
Lincoln Olbrycht
Sally Powers
Sue Smith
Ruby Tellsworth

Stockton City Unified School District
Jan Holloway

Vallejo City Unified School District
Howard Banford

Canada

School District No. 39, Vancouver, British Columbia
Shirley Brunke
Pat Craig
Joan Crockett
Wayne Gatley
Liz Gautschi
Linda O'Reilly
Jan Renouf
Carrie Sleep

The staff at Addison-Wesley was an additional source of guidance for us. In particular, we wish to thank the following:

M. Patricia Brill, Editorial Director
Michael Kane, Managing Editor
Mali Apple, Project Editor
Claire Flaherty, Production Coordinator

We wish to thank the past and present staff of the Developmental Studies Center, particularly the following people, for their support and invaluable contributions:

Eric Schaps, President
Anne Goddard, Publications Editor
Lynn Murphy, Publications Editor
Caroline Arakelian, Copy Editor
Susan Urquhart-Brown, Curriculum Developer
Patrick Kammermeyer, Computer Specialist
Joanne Slaboch, Director of Administration
Pam Herrera, Director of Administration
Dan Solomon, Director of Research
Carol Stone, Evaluator
Margaret Tauber, Evaluator
Denise Wood, Administrative Assistant

Finally, the publication of this book would not have been possible without the help of the current Cooperative Mathematics Project staff and consultants:

Susan Frost, Production Editor
Allan Ferguson, Computer Specialist
Stella McCloskey, Administrative Assistant
Duane Bibby, Illustrator

About the Authors

Laurel Robertson
Director

Dr. Robertson has been in education for more than twenty years as a classroom teacher, staff developer, mathematics consultant, and director of several educational programs. She is past president of the California Association for Cooperation in Education and is currently on the board of directors of the International Association for the Study of Cooperation in Education.

Shaila Regan
Co-Director/
Curriculum
Developer

Ms. Regan has extensive experience as an elementary school mathematics specialist and classroom teacher. She has also been a mathematics consultant and staff developer for public and private schools throughout the United States, and is past president of the Alameda/Contra Costa Counties Mathematics Educators.

Marji Freeman
Curriculum
Developer

Ms. Freeman has more than fifteen years' experience as a middle-school mathematics teacher and mathematics consultant. In 1986, she received the Texas State Presidential Award in Mathematics Teaching. Ms. Freeman is an instructor for Marilyn Burns Education Associates, consultant to Cuisenaire Company of America, and author of *Creative Graphing* (Cuisenaire Company of America, 1986).

Julie Wellington Contestable
Curriculum
Developer

Ms. Contestable has more than fifteen years' experience as an elementary classroom teacher, mentor for Language Arts and Mathematics, and mathematics specialist. She has been a leader in district and county mathematics committees and in California School Improvement Program reviews. She is an officer of the Alameda/Contra Costa Counties Mathematics Educators.

Preface

This is an exciting time to be a mathematics teacher. Educators and the general public alike are calling for fundamental changes in the content and process of mathematics instruction. Recent national reports document the need for change, describe new goals for the field, and suggest new approaches to teaching and learning.

Number Power is designed to meet the call for curricula that models new instructional strategies and content. The focus of the program is to support and expand students' emerging number sense. The *Number Power* program consists of three multiweek units each for kindergarten through sixth grade, and is intended to supplement or replace existing curricula aimed at developing number concepts.

The *Number Power* units provide opportunities for all students to construct and expand their understanding of number over time, as they engage in and reflect on experiences that help them make mathematical connections, employ mathematical tools, work with others to solve problems, and communicate about their thinking. The units are designed to be accessible to all students and to meet the needs of students with diverse backgrounds and experiences. Each unit fosters the development of several essential concepts and may include other areas of mathematics, such as measurement, geometry, and data analysis.

Number Power takes a holistic, developmental view of education and is designed to enhance students' social, as well as mathematical, development. Cooperative group work and ongoing discussion about group interaction help students understand the need to be fair, caring, and responsible, and develop the skills needed to work successfully with others.

Number Sense and Social Development

Number Power is based on the assumption that we learn about the world through everyday interaction with our environment and with others. Academic and social learning are integrated naturally, rather than developed in isolation from each other. Exploration, questioning, discussion, and reasoning are all part of this natural learning process that begins at birth.

With this assumption in mind, *Number Power* has been designed to support students' mathematical and social development in an integrated manner by actively engaging them in exploration and reasoning with others. Students in pairs and in groups investigate open-ended questions; use a wide variety of tools; develop problem-solving strategies; collect, organize, and analyze data; and record and communicate their thinking and results. Students' sense of number is fostered along with their understanding of what it means to be fair, caring, and responsible and their disposition and ability to act on these values.

Number Sense

A sound understanding of number is indispensible to making sense of the world. Documents such as *Curriculum and Evaluation Standards for School Mathematics* (National Council of Teachers of Mathematics, 1989) and *Reshaping School Mathematics* (Mathematical Sciences Education Board, 1990) make it clear that the development of students' number sense should be a primary goal of elementary school mathematics programs.

The focus of *Number Power* is to develop students' number sense. In particular, the program is designed to enhance students' understanding of number meaning and relationships, the relative magnitude of number, the effects and relative relationships of operations, and referents for quantities and measures. *Number Power* is also designed to enhance students' abilities to apply these concepts to everyday problems.

Students come to school with some understanding of the meaning of numbers, of how numbers relate to each other, and of how numbers can be used to describe quantities. *Number Power* extends this conceptual understanding by providing opportunities for students to explore and use numbers as they solve problems, discuss their thinking, and make connections between their experience and the underlying concepts.

This cycle of concrete experiences and reflection on these experiences also enhances students' sense of the relative magnitude of whole numbers, decimals, and fractions. Students begin to understand, for example, that 24 is two twelves, almost 25, about half of 50, small compared with 93, and large compared with 3. They also begin to develop "benchmarks"—recognizing, for example, that 0.8 is closer to 1.0 than to 0.5.

Number Power strives to deepen students' understanding of how operations affect numbers—how, for example, adding 4 to 24 results in a far smaller change in the number than does multiplying 24 by 4. Students have opportunities to develop their own algorithms and to begin to develop a sense of the effect of using a number as an operator on other numbers—understanding, for example, what happens when a number is multiplied by 0 or divided by 1.

Number Power involves students in experiences that help them relate numbers to the real world. As a result of experiences such as these, students begin to develop appropriate referents for numbers used in everyday life and to develop a range of possible quantities and measures for everyday situations. They begin to recognize, for example, that a dog would not weigh 800 pounds or that it is reasonable that a new car would cost about $15,000.

Number Power provides opportunities for students to apply their understanding of number to problems and to everyday situations. Students collect, organize, and interpret data, and develop their own informal ways to compute. Within a variety of problem-solving and real-life contexts—such as cooking, surveying class members about their pets, or making a quilt—students are encouraged to

- make estimates;
- decide when an estimate or an exact answer is appropriate;
- make sense of numbers and judge the reasonableness of solutions;
- use numbers to support an argument; and
- make decisions about the appropriate use of different computational methods—calculator, pencil and paper, or mental computation.

Social Development

Traditionally, schools have taken a major role in the socialization of students, helping them become responsible citizens. In recent decades, this role has taken a backseat to academic preparation, as students and schools have been judged almost entirely by their success in meeting narrow academic standards.

Today, however, the stresses of our rapidly changing world require schools to refocus attention on students' social development while continuing to support their academic development. In order to prepare students for the challenges of the next century, schools must help them

- be creative, thoughtful, and knowledgeable;
- develop a lifelong love of learning and the ability to pursue their own learning goals;
- be principled, responsible, and humane; and
- be able to work effectively with others to solve problems.

The recognition that social development and academic learning are integral to schooling and occur simultaneously is a cornerstone of *Number Power*. In each lesson, students have opportunities to explore and solve problems with others and to discuss and reflect on their group interaction. In the process, students are encouraged to balance their own needs with the needs of others, to recognize how their behavior affects others, to think about the underlying values that guide behavior, and to develop appropriate group skills. Reflection on their experience helps students construct their understanding of social and cultural norms, and leads to a deeper integration of positive social values in their lives.

Using Cooperative Group Work in Your Classroom

Cooperative group work benefits all students, both academically and socially. When students with different abilities, backgrounds, and perspectives explain their thinking and listen to the thinking of others, their reasoning and communication skills are fostered. Additionally, they are exposed to new ideas and strategies, learn to be supportive of and to value others, and become more positive about themselves as learners and more motivated to learn.

What Is the *Number Power* Approach?

The *Number Power* approach to cooperative group work includes some elements common to most cooperative learning methods: students work in heterogeneous pairs or groups as they pursue a common goal, are actively involved in their learning, and have ongoing opportunities to share ideas, discuss their thinking, and hear the thinking of others.

The *Number Power* approach differs from other cooperative learning methods in several respects, but especially in its focus on social development. Beyond addressing group skills, *Number Power* places particular emphasis on encouraging students to be responsible for their own learning and behavior, and on helping students construct their understanding of

- what it means to be fair, caring, and responsible;
- why these values are important; and
- how these values can be acted on in their daily lives.

Another difference is that the *Number Power* approach does not specify role assignments for group work. Instead, the lessons provide opportunities for students to decide such things as how they will divide the work or how they will record and report their findings. Learning how to make these decisions helps students become responsible group members. Many of the lessons include examples of questions that help students think about how they made these decisions and what

they learned that would help them the next time they work together.

The *Number Power* approach does not recommend that student work be graded. The goal of the lessons is to support conceptual development. The lessons are designed to be learning experiences rather than experiences that expect student mastery and strive to encourage exploration, creativity, and intrinsic motivation. Concern about grades can greatly inhibit students' willingness to take risks and explore alternative strategies. *Number Power* lessons do, however, provide many opportunities for ongoing assessment of student understanding.

Throughout all aspects of the *Number Power* lessons, the asking of probing, open-ended questions is paramount to helping students construct their understanding. The questions suggested in the lessons seldom have a single right answer. Many are focused on helping students examine and rely on the authority of their own thinking. If students are used to answering recall questions or to giving an answer that they think the teacher wants, they may initially fail to understand the questions or meet them with silence or irrelevant answers. Their willingness to risk will increase as they understand that explaining their thinking and sharing many strategies and solutions is valued and important. Their ability to explain their thinking will increase with practice.

Many of the *Number Power* lessons suggest the use of some easily implemented cooperative learning strategies that provide opportunities for students to share their thinking. (For more information about cooperative strategies, Kagan's *Cooperative*

Learning is particularly informative. See Additional Reading, p. 191.)

1. *Turn to Your Partner.* Students turn to a person sitting next to them to discuss an issue or question.

2. *Heads Together.* Students in groups of four put their heads together to discuss an issue or question among themselves.

3. *Think, Pair, Share.* Students individually take a short period of time to think about a question or issue and then discuss their thoughts with a partner. The pair reports its thinking to another pair or to the class.

4. *Think, Pair, Write.* This structure is like "Think, Pair, Share," except the pairs write about their thinking after they have discussed their thoughts. This writing then might be shared with you, with another pair, or with the class.

5. *Group Brainstorming.* In this structure, each group needs someone to record ideas. Groups are given some time to come up with as many ideas as they can about a topic or a problem, and the recorder lists all ideas. Then groups are given time to analyze, synthesize, and prioritize their ideas.

The *Number Power* approach recognizes that a strong mathematics program will include a variety of instructional methods. The program, therefore, includes some direct instruction and individual work in addition to cooperative group work.

How Are *Number Power* Lessons Structured?

Number Power lessons are structured to provide frequent opportunities for students to interact with each other and with the teacher. Group work and class discussion alternate throughout the lessons. Many lessons begin with a class discussion about such things as the goals of the lesson and how they fit with previous work, the mathematical and social emphases of the lesson, and the problem or activity. During group work, students are asked open-ended questions to extend their thinking, to help them

solve problems, or to informally assess their concept development. At times, the class meets to discuss strategies and solutions, and often new questions. The lesson concludes with an opportunity for groups and the class to reflect on their mathematical work and social interaction.

How Do I Begin?

Whether or not you have used cooperative learning strategies before, it is a good idea to start slowly. Begin with pairs rather than larger group sizes. Try some of the cooperative learning strategies suggested in the previous section. These and other strategies can be used as part of the teaching and learning experience in any subject and can be used to structure student interaction before, during, and after traditional or cooperative lessons.

An important factor in helping students become responsible, independent, and cooperative learners is the establishment of an environment that supports cooperation. A supportive environment makes students feel safe, values and respects their efforts and opinions, and provides them with many opportunities to make choices and decisions. The role you play and what you model are crucial to the development of this environment. For example, asking questions that help students solve a problem on their own encourages them to become responsible for their learning and shows that you value their ability to do so. Asking open-ended questions beginning with such words as what, why, or how helps students extend their understanding and become confident in their abilities. Likewise, asking for a variety of solutions to a problem and for explanations of how they were derived helps students understand that risk-taking is desirable, that you are not just looking for a "right" answer, and that you value their thinking. Also, encouraging students to respectfully ask each other questions about their strategies creates a safe environment for constructive disagreement.

The physical setup of the room is also an important factor. The arrangement should allow group members to have access to materials and to be able to communicate with each other easily. Sharing one desk or small table, or sitting at two desks side-by-side, is a good arrangement for a pair; a small table or a cluster of desks works well for a group of four.

Learning to cooperate is a developmental process and can be difficult for students, especially in the beginning. Students may, for example, have trouble balancing their own needs with those of others, taking responsibility for their work and behavior, or dealing with open-ended questions. Understanding that these difficulties are a valuable part of the learning process will help both you and your students be more comfortable.

Class Building

At the beginning of the year in particular, it is important to help students develop a sense of identity and community as a group in order to support and develop a sense of cooperation. Students need ongoing opportunities to learn about each other, to set norms for behavior, and to make decisions about their classroom. Activities such as developing a class name, logo, or handshake can lead to an "our classroom" feeling. (Many ideas for class-building activities can be found in such resources as Graves' *A Part to Play*, Mormon and Dishon's *Our Classroom*, Rhodes and McCabe's *The Nurturing Classroom*, and Gibbs and Allen's *Tribes*. See Additional Reading, p. 191.)

Class building is an ongoing process; the spirit of community needs to be developed and supported throughout the year. Class-building activities are particularly important after a long vacation, after you have been absent for an extended period of time, after illness has kept many students home, or when you have an influx of new students.

Forming Groups

Several decisions need to be made regarding group formation: the size of the groups, how to form them, and how long to keep them together. The *Number Power* program suggests a group size for each lesson, and that students be randomly assigned to groups that work together for an entire unit.

A major benefit of randomly assigning students to groups is that it gives several positive messages to students: there is no hidden agenda behind how you grouped students (such as choosing groups based on student achievement); every student is considered a valuable group member; and everyone is expected to learn to work with everyone

else. Randomly assigning students also results in heterogenous groups, important for cooperative group work, even though at times a group may be homogenous in some way; for example, all girls or all boys. The following are several ways to randomly group students. (Other suggestions can be found in the Johnsons' *Circle of Learning*. See Additional Reading, p. 191.)

1. Have students number off and have the ones form a group, the twos form a group, and so on.

2. Have students take a playing card or an ice cream stick with a number on it and find others with the same number.

3. Have students take a card with an equation or short word problem on it and form a group with others who have an equation or word problem with the same solution.

4. Cut magazine pictures into the same number of pieces as members in a group. Have students pick a piece and find others with pieces of the same puzzle.

Keeping groups together for an entire unit provides an opportunity for students to develop and expand their interpersonal skills and their understanding of group interaction. Students learn to work through and learn from problems, and to build on successful methods of interaction. Long-term group work also allows students to build on their mathematical discoveries.

Team Building

Each time new long-term groups are formed, it is important to provide opportunities for students to get better acquainted, to develop a sense of identity as a team, and to begin to develop their working relationship. Each *Number Power* unit begins with a team-building activity. (The references suggested under Class Building also are good sources for additional team-building activities.)

During team-building activities, helping students label, discuss, and analyze behavior lays a foundation for their future group work. Open-ended questions can draw students' attention to their interaction, to their behavior that helps the group, and to how they might solve problems that have arisen.

Such questions might, for example, encourage students to talk about how they worked together; what group skills they used; how they wish to treat each other; why it is important to be fair, caring, and responsible; what problems they had; and the ways they wish to work together the next time.

What Is My Role?

One of the main goals of cooperative group work is to encourage students to do their own thinking and to take responsibility for their own learning. Your role is vital to the process of students becoming independent and interdependent learners. In addition to setting the environment for cooperation, this role includes planning and introducing the lesson, facilitating group work, helping students reflect, and helping students say good-bye.

Planning

Reading a *Number Power* unit, Overview and lessons, prior to implementation will help you make decisions about how to connect the lessons with students' previous experiences, and about the social values and group skills that might be emphasized throughout the unit. The group skills listed on the first page of each lesson are suggestions based on the type of student interaction that might occur in that lesson. (Listening skills, for example, might be the focus of a lesson in which students are explaining their thinking to others.) However, the developmental level of your students, their previous cooperative group experiences, and level of cooperation they demonstrate may lead you to choose other skills as a focus. You might also wish to develop a theme for a unit, such as communicating with others.

The following list of questions may help you as you plan. The *Number Power* lessons incorporate suggestions for many of them.

- What are the important *mathematical concepts* of the lesson? How are they linked with previous work and long-term goals?
- What are some possible opportunities for supporting social, as well as mathematical, learning?
- Is the lesson *interesting, accessible,* and *challenging* for all students? What modifications are needed?

- What *room arrangement* will be best for the lesson?
- What *materials* will be needed for the lesson?
- How will time for *student discussion* and *work* be maximized?
- How will *interdependence* among group members be encouraged?
- How will the lesson provide opportunities for students to *make decisions* and *take responsibility* for their learning and behavior?
- What will you be looking for as you *observe* group work?
- What *open-ended questions* might extend students' thinking?
- How will *assessment* be linked with instruction?
- What are appropriate *extension activities* for groups that finish early or for the next day?

Introducing the Lesson

Many *Number Power* lessons begin with questions that ask students to reflect on previous lessons or experiences, or pose a problem for students to discuss. Such questions are often followed with discussion about a problem or investigation that students will undertake and about specific cooperative group skills that might help them work effectively.

Discussing group skills at the beginning of the lesson provides students with models for positive interaction and with language to discuss their interaction. Vary the way these group skills are discussed. You might choose, for example, to emphasize a skill such as listening to others, then have students discuss what it means to listen, how others will know that they are being listened to, how listening might help their group work, and how listening to others relates to the values of being fair, caring, and responsible. You might, instead, ask groups to discuss and choose skills that they think are important to the functioning of their group, or ask students to discuss what they have learned about working together that will help them in this new lesson. At other times, you could have students role-play the activity and then, as a class, discuss what they observed about the group interaction and what group skills they think might be particularly important to their work. For some lessons, you might choose not to discuss group interaction at all during the introduction. No matter how and when you choose to discuss the social emphases of the lesson and the group skills with students, it is important to remember that social understanding is constructed through many opportunities to work with others and reflect on their experience.

Facilitating Group Work

During group work, ask thoughtful, probing, open-ended questions. The focus of such questions is to help students define the problems they are investigating, to help them solve interpersonal problems, to help them take responsibility for their learning and behavior, and to extend and informally assess their thinking.

As students begin group work, observe each group to be sure that students have understood the task and have no insurmountable problems; then focus on a few groups and observe each of them long enough to see what is really happening. This will provide you with information about students' ability to work together, their involvement in the activity, and their mathematical and social understanding. Such observation will also give you ideas for questions you might ask, and help you determine what other experiences students may need.

At times during group work, you may decide to intervene to refocus a group, to help them see a problem from another perspective, to ask questions that extend mathematical and social learning, or to assess understanding. When you intervene to assess or extend thinking, try not to interrupt the flow of the group work. Wait for a natural pause in the action. Ask open-ended questions that require progressively more thought or understanding. (Each *Number Power* lesson suggests sample questions to probe students' thinking about number and number relationships, to help them think about how they are solving problems, and to help them analyze their group work.) If a group is having difficulty, allow members time to solve a problem themselves before you intervene. Then, ask key questions to help them resolve the difficulty, rather than solving the problem for them or giving lengthy explanations.

Helping Students Reflect

Reflection on the mathematical and social aspects of group work helps students develop their conceptual understanding, build on past learning experiences, and connect their experience to long-term learning goals. Questioning before, during, and after group work encourages students to consider such important issues as, "What does it mean to be responsible?" and "How did my behavior affect others in the group?" and extends their mathematical thinking. *Number Power* lessons incorporate several methods to structure ongoing reflection, including group discussion, writing, and whole-class discussions. Each *Number Power* unit ends with a transition lesson to provide students with an opportunity to reflect on their mathematical work and group interaction during the unit.

Helping Students Say Good-Bye

When it is time to disband groups that have been working together for some time, it is important to provide opportunities for students to express their feelings and to say good-bye. The transition lessons at the end of each *Number Power* unit are designed for this purpose. You may wish to do some other parting activities, such as:

1. *Group Memories Bulletin Board.* Have groups write favorite memories about their group work or about each other and then post them on a bulletin board labeled "Group Memories."

2. *Group Memory Books.* Have groups make a book that includes work from their favorite investigations, comments from each member about what they liked about the unit and working together with each other, and a picture or drawing of the group.

3. *Thank-You Letters.* Have group members write thank-you letters to each other expressing appreciation for something specific.

4. *Good-bye Celebrations.* Have each group plan a way to celebrate their work together.

(For ideas for parting or closing activities, see Rhodes and McCabe's *The Nurturing Classroom* and Gibbs and Allen's *Tribes*. See Additional Reading, p. 191.)

Number Power Format

The *Number Power* program for Grade 3 consists of three units of eight to ten lessons each. In Unit 1, students explore the composition and decomposition of numbers into ones, tens and hundreds and place value concepts. They compute with multiples of tens and hundreds, explore the relative magnitude of two- and three-digit numbers, and use play money to solve problems, play games, and write and solve riddles. The focus of Unit 2 is to help students develop and use strategies for mental computation, and to further develop their ability to compose and decompose numbers. Unit 3 provides opportunities for students to explore numbers and choose ways to calculate as they collect, organize, and interpret data. This unit also integrates literature and provides opportunities for student research.

The *Number Power* program for Grade 3 additionally fosters students' ability to take responsibility for their learning and behavior and to analyze how their behavior affects others, their group interaction, and their group work. Throughout the units, students are encouraged to develop group skills, particularly their ability to explain their thinking, help others, and to reach agreements that both partners find acceptable.

Unit Format

Each unit includes an Overview, a class-building or team-building lesson, conceptual lessons, and a transition lesson.

Overview

The Overview will acquaint you with the unit and offer suggestions for implementation. This section provides a synopsis of all the lessons, a discussion of the major mathematical concepts and social understandings that the lessons help students develop, and a list of all the materials you will need for the unit. The Overview also includes a discussion of informal assessment techniques you might use throughout the unit, and a summary of the specific types of student writing opportunities in the unit.

Team-Building Lessons

Each unit begins with a team-building lesson to help group members become acquainted, to begin to develop their sense of unity, and to develop their group skills. These lessons also focus on developing students' understanding of why these skills are important for the effective functioning of their group. You may wish to do more than the one team-building lesson suggested. Other ideas can be found in *A Part to Play, Tribes, Our Classroom*, and *The Nurturing Classroom* (listed in Additional Reading, p. 191).

Conceptual Lessons

The lessons that follow the team-building lessons focus on developing and extending students' sense of number through a variety of cooperative problem-solving experiences. Students use materials such as dice, spinners, play money, and Hundred Charts to explore the composition and decomposition of numbers, place value, and relative magnitude, and to develop strategies for mental computation. The lessons also provide opportunities for students to develop their abilities to work together effectively and to reflect on their mathematical and social experience.

Transition Lessons

Each unit ends with a transition lesson that encourages students to reflect on their mathematical work throughout the unit and to make generalizations and connections. This lesson is also designed to encourage students to think about their group interaction, their successes and problems, and the things they have learned that will help them in future group work.

In addition to this reflection, the transition lesson allows students to express appreciation for each other and to celebrate their work together. After students have worked as a group for a period of time, it may be difficult for them to face separation and move to a new group; the transition lesson gives students a chance to make this break more easily by giving them time to acknowledge their attachment to their group and providing ways to say good-bye.

Lesson Format

First Page

The first page provides you with the logistical information you need for the lesson.

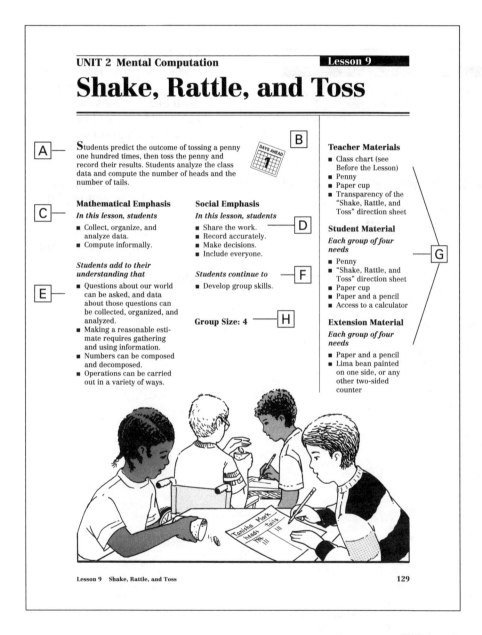

UNIT 2 Mental Computation   Lesson 9

Shake, Rattle, and Toss

A — **S**tudents predict the outcome of tossing a penny one hundred times, then toss the penny and record their results. Students analyze the class data and compute the number of heads and the number of tails.

B

Mathematical Emphasis
C — *In this lesson, students*
- Collect, organize, and analyze data.
- Compute informally.

Students add to their understanding that
E —
- Questions about our world can be asked, and data about those questions can be collected, organized, and analyzed.
- Making a reasonable estimate requires gathering and using information.
- Numbers can be composed and decomposed.
- Operations can be carried out in a variety of ways.

Social Emphasis
In this lesson, students
- Share the work.   — D
- Record accurately.
- Make decisions.
- Include everyone.

Students continue to   — F
- Develop group skills.

Group Size: 4 — H

Teacher Materials
- Class chart (see Before the Lesson)
- Penny
- Paper cup
- Transparency of the "Shake, Rattle, and Toss" direction sheet

Student Material
Each group of four needs
- Penny
- "Shake, Rattle, and Toss" direction sheet
- Paper cup
- Paper and a pencil
- Access to a calculator

G

Extension Material
Each group of four needs
- Paper and a pencil
- Lima bean painted on one side, or any other two-sided counter

Lesson 9 Shake, Rattle, and Toss   129

Notice the lesson summary (A). Next to the summary you will often see an icon (B). This alerts you that something needs your attention prior to the lesson or that the lesson has a special focus: team-building or transition.

The first page details the dual emphasis of the lesson. It lists the mathematical and social emphases (C and D), as well as the essential mathematical and social concepts the lesson helps develop (E and F). (See Planning, p. xiv, for a discussion about choosing group skills.)

On the first page you will also find a list of the materials specific to the lesson (G) and the suggested group size (H). *It is assumed that calculators and manipulative materials are available to students at all times for use at their discretion, and that the materials listed for students are available to groups or pairs in their work area at the start of the lesson, unless otherwise indicated in a lesson.*

Interior Pages

Some lessons begin with a section titled Before the Lesson (I). This section suggests student activities or material preparation that you may need to undertake prior to the lesson.

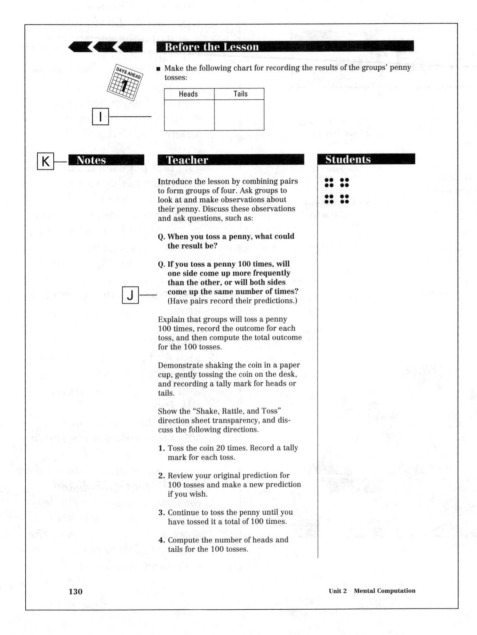

The lesson is divided into three columns. The center column (J) is the lesson plan itself and includes sample open-ended questions to probe and extend students' thinking.

The left column (K) provides notes and suggestions for you. In some lessons, this column also contains an assessment icon (L) accompanied by suggestions for informal assessment.
See the following page for examples.

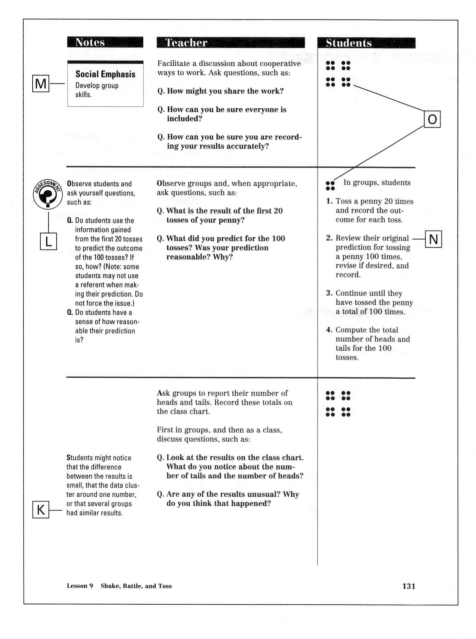

Notes

Social Emphasis
Develop group skills.

Observe students and ask yourself questions, such as:

Q. Do students use the information gained from the first 20 tosses to predict the outcome of the 100 tosses? If so, how? (Note: some students may not use a referent when making their prediction. Do not force the issue.)

Q. Do students have a sense of how reasonable their prediction is?

Students might notice that the difference between the results is small, that the data cluster around one number, or that several groups had similar results.

Teacher

Facilitate a discussion about cooperative ways to work. Ask questions, such as:

Q. How might you share the work?

Q. How can you be sure everyone is included?

Q. How can you be sure you are recording your results accurately?

Observe groups and, when appropriate, ask questions, such as:

Q. What is the result of the first 20 tosses of your penny?

Q. What did you predict for the 100 tosses? Was your prediction reasonable? Why?

Ask groups to report their number of heads and tails. Record these totals on the class chart.

First in groups, and then as a class, discuss questions, such as:

Q. Look at the results on the class chart. What do you notice about the number of tails and the number of heads?

Q. Are any of the results unusual? Why do you think that happened?

Students

In groups, students

1. Toss a penny 20 times and record the outcome for each toss.

2. Review their original prediction for tossing a penny 100 times, revise if desired, and record.

3. Continue until they have tossed the penny a total of 100 times.

4. Compute the total number of heads and tails for the 100 tosses.

The boxes (M) suggest important mathematical and social concepts as the focus of your open-ended questions in that portion of the lesson.

The right column (N) describes the student work. It includes icons (O), described below, that indicate how the students are grouped for each section of the lesson.

Group Size Icons

Whole class icons

Teacher talks with the whole class, prior to grouping students, or after group work is complete.

Teacher talks with the whole class, already in groups of four.

Teacher talks with the whole class, already in pairs.

Student work icons

Students work in groups of four.

Students work in pairs.

Students work individually.

Last Page— Extensions

It seems to be a law of nature that cooperative groups seldom finish their work at the same time. To help manage this and to further students' conceptual development, two additional types of activities are included at the end of each lesson.

The first, "For Pairs [or Groups] That Finish Early" (P), suggests activities for groups to engage in as other groups complete their lesson work. The second, "For the Next Day" (Q), further develops concepts or gives students more experience with the same concepts before moving on to the next lesson in the unit. Some of the activities foster students' social, as well as academic, learning.

Notes	Teacher	Students

Notes

Encourage groups to compute mentally or to use informal strategies for finding the total number of heads and tails. For example, some groups might add a column of numbers by first adding all the compatible numbers, and some groups might add pairs of numbers and combine the sums (with or without a calculator) to find the total. Other groups might add the numbers in the 10s column first and then add the 1s. Write the groups' strategies where all can see and discuss them. Have students try each other's strategies.

Teacher

Q. How many of the total number of tosses were tails?

Q. What strategy did your group use to compute the number of tails? Did any group use a different strategy?

Q. How many of the total number of tosses were heads?

Q. What strategy did your group use to compute the number of heads? Did any group use a different strategy?

Help students reflect on the group work. Ask questions, such as:

Q. What decisions did your group make before you began to toss the penny? How did that affect your work?

Q. What did you like about the way your group worked?

Extensions

For Groups That Finish Early

■ Have students discuss and solve the following problem:

If each student in the class tossed a coin 100 times, how many tosses would the class make? — P

For the Next Day

■ Give each group a lima bean painted on one side (or any other two-sided counter) and ask: "If you toss the lima bean 100 times, will one side come up more frequently than the other? Will both sides come up the same number of times? What do you think will happen? Why?" — Q

Have groups

1. Predict the outcome of tossing the lima bean 100 times and record the prediction.

2. Toss the lima bean 100 times and record the outcome for each toss.

3. Compute the total number of times each side comes up.

4. Compare the prediction for the 100 tosses with the actual outcome.

5. Discuss how this activity is similar to or different from the penny toss activity in Lesson 8.

Exploring Tens and Hundreds

Mathematical Development

This unit provides opportunities for students to continue to construct their understanding of tens and hundreds. In many lessons, students use play money to explore and develop concepts. Students informally explore the decomposition of tens and hundreds in different ways; compute with multiples of ten and one hundred; group and regroup tens and hundreds; and explore the relative magnitude of numbers and number patterns. Students also explore two- and three-digit numbers in real-life contexts, and write and solve number riddles.

Although Unit 1 was designed to precede Unit 2, you might wish to switch the order of these units. Unit 1 provides students with many experiences composing and decomposing numbers. These experiences provide a conceptual foundation for the development of mental computation strategies. If, however, your students are comfortable decomposing numbers into ones, tens, and hundreds, you might choose to begin the year with Unit 2. The social interaction in Unit 2, due to its mathematical focus on mental computation, is less complex than that in Unit 1. Unit 2 also begins with a team-building activity that is quite appropriate for the beginning of the school year.

Social Development

This unit provides opportunities for students to examine how they might take responsibility for their own learning and behavior and to analyze how their behavior and the behavior of others affects their group work and interaction. Students discuss ways to work with a partner to solve problems, to reach agreements, to explain their thinking, and to share work. Open-ended questions encourage students to focus on how their behavior relates to the values of fairness, caring, and responsibility.

Students should be randomly assigned to pairs that work together throughout the unit. In Lessons 1 and 7, pairs combine to work in groups of four. In Lesson 4, students work in groups of four.

Mathematical Emphasis

Conceptually, experiences in this unit help students construct their understanding that

- Numbers can be composed and decomposed.
- Numbers can be used to describe quantities.
- The relative magnitude of numbers can be described.
- Our place value system is based on an organizational structure of grouping and regrouping.
- Problems may have more than one solution and may be solved in a variety of ways.
- Making a reasonable estimate requires gathering and using information.
- Once a rule to generate a pattern has been identified, the pattern can usually be extended.

Social Emphasis

Socially, experiences in this unit help students to

- Develop group skills.
- Analyze the effect of behavior on others and on the group work.
- Relate the values of fairness, caring, and responsibility to behavior.

Lessons

This unit includes eight lessons, an ongoing bulletin board activity, and an ongoing mental computation activity. The calendar icon indicates that some preparation is needed or that an experience is suggested for the students prior to that lesson.

1. What's the Number?
(page 11)

Introductory team-building lesson that encourages cooperation between partners as they write clues describing two- or three-digit numbers.

2. Our Classroom
(page 21)

Estimation lesson in which pairs write statements about objects in the classroom.

3. Is It Close?
(page 25)

Spinner activity in which pairs find sums and determine their relative magnitude.

4. One Thousand Dollars
(page 35)

Trading game in which groups of four exchange sums of money until they reach the goal of $1000.

5. Bank Teller
(page 45)

Problem-solving lesson in which pairs decompose amounts of money in many different ways.

6. It's a Riddle!
(page 53)

Problem-solving lesson in which pairs solve number riddles.

7. Riddle Book
(page 59)

Problem-solving lesson in which pairs write number riddles and contribute them to a class book.

8. The Crazy ATM
(page 63)

Transition lesson in which pairs design a crazy automatic teller machine and reflect on their work together.

"Numbers in Our World" Bulletin Board

This ongoing activity provides opportunities for students to explore numbers in real-life contexts. Throughout the unit, ask students to collect newspaper and magazine advertisements and headlines that show examples of two- and three-digit numbers. Post these examples on a bulletin board titled "Numbers in Our World." Frequently refer to the information in the clippings, and ask students to discuss whether they think the numbers are estimates or exact and how the magnitude of the numbers relate to other posted numbers. This ongoing activity begins in Lesson 1, first with directions for students to collect examples at home and at school, then continues in the Extension For the Next Day.

Base Ten Activities

These ongoing visualization and mental computation activities help students develop a mental image of manageable sets of numbers and enable them to mentally manipulate, compose, and decompose those sets of numbers.

These short, teacher-directed activities are to be repeated many times throughout the unit. For each activity, use an overhead projector and a set of overhead base ten blocks or a set of transparent base ten blocks (see Base Ten Activities blackline master, p. 9).

Activity 1

Show 20 ones in a random pile on the overhead for about five seconds (see Diagram 1) and ask:

Diagram 1

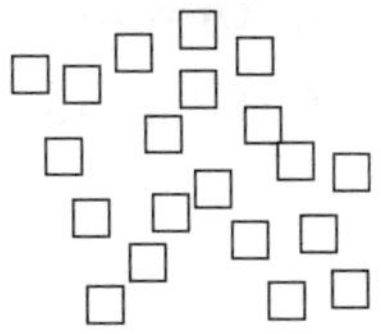

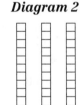

> Q. How many blocks do you see?
>
> Q. Is it difficult to know the number? Why?
>
> Q. How could we organize the blocks to easily recognize the number of blocks?

Count the blocks. Organize the ones into sets of ten and facilitate a discussion about which is easier to count, the pile of 20 ones or the two sets of ten. Exchange the 20 ones for 2 tens rods and establish that the 2 tens rods represent the number 20.

Activity 2

Show 3 tens rods on the overhead for about five seconds. (See Diagram 2.) Turn off the overhead projector and ask:

Diagram 2

> Q. How many tens? (3) What is the number? (30)

With the overhead projector off, add 2 tens and 3 ones. (See Diagram 3.) Turn on the overhead for about five seconds, then turn off the overhead and ask:

Diagram 3

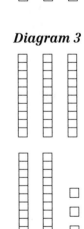

> Q. Now what's the number? (53) How do you know? How many tens and ones were added to 30 to make 53? (2 tens, 3 ones)

Take away 4 tens and 2 ones. (See Diagram 4.) Turn on the overhead for about five seconds, then turn off the overhead and ask:

Diagram 4

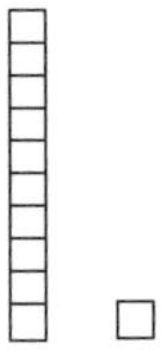

> Q. What is the number? (11) How do you know? How many tens and ones? (1 ten, 1 one)

Repeat this activity using many different two- and three-digit numbers.

Activity 3

Show a ten and 2 ones on the overhead. (See Diagram 5.) State that the number represented by the blocks is 12, and ask:

Q. How many tens do I need to add to 12 to make 62? (5)
How do you know?

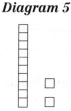

Diagram 5

With the overhead on, add 5 tens (see Diagram 6) and ask:

Q. What is the number? (62)

Q. How many tens did I add to 12? (5 tens)

Q. What number did I add to 12 to make 62? (50 or 5 tens)

Repeat this activity using many different two- and three-digit numbers.

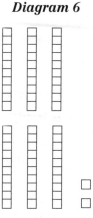

Diagram 6

Activity 4

Show 3 tens and 4 ones on the overhead for about five seconds. (See Diagram 7.) Turn off the overhead and ask:

Q. What is the number? (34) **How many tens and ones?** (3 tens, 4 ones)

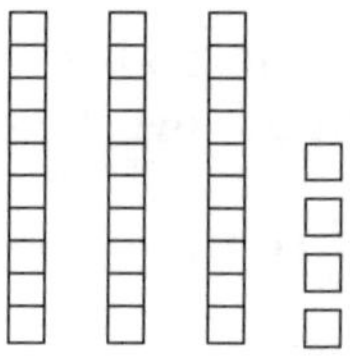

Have students close their eyes and picture these base ten blocks. Ask:

Q. How many tens and ones would I need to take away from 34 to make 12? (2 tens, 2 ones) **What is that number?** (22)

Turn on the overhead and take away 2 tens and 2 ones. (See Diagram 8.)

Repeat this activity using many different two-digit numbers.

Diagram 7

Diagram 8

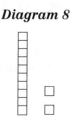

Activity 5

Show 5 hundred blocks on the overhead for about five seconds. (See Diagram 9.) Turn off the overhead and ask:

Q. What is the number? (500) **How many hundred blocks?** (5)

Diagram 9

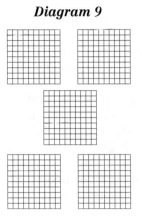

Add 4 tens and 2 ones. (See Diagram 10.) Show the blocks on the overhead for about five seconds. Turn off the overhead and ask:

Q. What is the number? (542) **How do you know? How many hundreds, tens, and ones?** (5 hundreds, 4 tens, 2 ones)

Repeat this activity using many different numbers.

Diagram 10

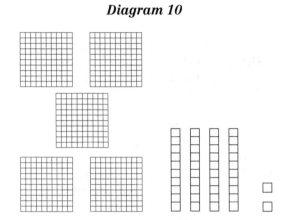

Materials

The materials needed for the unit are listed below. The first page of each lesson lists the materials specific to that lesson. All blackline masters for transparencies and group record sheets are included at the end of each lesson. These and many other materials are available in the *Number Power* Package for Grade 3.

Throughout the unit, you will need access to an overhead projector, and students will need access to supplies such as calculators, scissors, crayons, markers, rulers, glue sticks, paper, and pencils. If possible, each group should have a container with these supplies available for their use at their discretion. The Hundred Chart and the Two-Hundred Chart blackline masters are located at the end of Lesson 1. The Count by Tens Chart blackline master is located at the end of Lesson 3. Use these blackline masters to make copies and transparencies for lessons in Units 1, 2, and 3.

Teacher Materials

- Materials for Base Ten Activities (see p. 3)
- Bulletin board space for "Numbers in Our World" bulletin board activity
- Materials for forming pairs (Lesson 1)
- Transparency of "What's the Number?" clue sheet (Lesson 1)
- Examples of two- and three-digit numbers from newspapers and magazines (Lesson 1)
- Bulletin board space (Lesson 2)
- Four 5″ × 8½″ sheets of tagboard (Lesson 2)
- 2 overhead spinners (Lesson 3)
- Transparency of "Is It Close?" group record sheet (Lesson 3)
- Transparencies of One Thousand Dollars trading mat and play money (Lesson 4)
- Sentence strips (Lesson 6)
- Transparency of "It's a Riddle!" group record sheet (Lesson 6)
- Transparency of "The Crazy ATM Story" blackline master (Lesson 8)
- Transparency of "The Crazy ATM" direction sheet (Lesson 8)

Student Materials

Each student needs

- Examples of two- and three-digit numbers from newspapers and magazines (Lesson 2)
- One Thousand Dollars trading mat (Lesson 4)
- Envelope of play money (Lesson 4)

Each pair needs

- Hundred Chart (Lesson 1)
- Two-Hundred Chart (Lesson 1)
- 4 sentence strips (Lesson 2)

Student Materials *(continued)*

- 2 spinners (Lesson 3)
- Count by Tens Chart (Lesson 3)
- "Is It Close?" group record sheet (Lesson 3)
- Envelope of play money (Lessons 5, 6, 7, and 8)
- "It's a Riddle!" group record sheet (Lesson 6)

Each group of four needs

- Thousand-dollar play money bill (Lesson 4)
- 2 special dice (Lesson 4)
- Paper plate (Lesson 4)

Extension Materials

- Four 8½″ × 11″ signs (Lesson 3)
- Number cards (Lesson 5)

Each student needs

- Examples of two- and three-digit numbers from newspapers and magazines (Lessons 1 and 4)

Each pair needs

- Sentence strip (Lesson 2)
- Self-stick notes (Lessons 2 and 3)
- Calculator (Lesson 2)
- Number card (Lesson 3)
- Count by Tens Chart (Lesson 3)
- "Make It Large" place value mat and number cards (Lesson 5)
- "It's a Riddle! Extension" group record sheet (Lesson 6)
- "The Crazy ATM: Extension" group record sheet (Lesson 8)

Each group of four needs

- One Thousand Dollars game materials (Lessons 4, 6, and 7)
- Special die (Lesson 7)

Teaching Hints

- Prior to each lesson, think about open-ended questions you might ask to extend and probe the thinking of your students. Decide which Extensions to have ready when pairs finish early.

- Provide time for students to freely explore unfamiliar or infrequently used materials before a lesson.

- In this unit, students are frequently asked to explain their thinking to their partners and to the class. Many lessons suggest that you encourage students to verbalize their thinking and that you ask follow-up questions to help them more fully articulate their understanding. Recognize, however, that some students will have difficulty doing so, particularly at the beginning of the year. Provide many opportunities for students to not only talk about their thinking and to hear the thinking of others but to model, illustrate, or demonstrate their thinking.

- In this unit several games are introduced that enhance students' sense of number. For example, the games in Lesson 3 and in the Extension for Lesson 5 help students explore the relative magnitude of numbers. The game in Lesson 4 helps students explore the place value concepts of grouping and regrouping. Make the games available to students to play during their free time and as Extensions. Students will benefit from playing these games throughout the year.

- After each lesson, review any Extensions that students have not explored and decide whether to have students investigate these Extensions before going on to the next lesson.

Assessment Techniques

These informal techniques will help you assess your students' understanding of grouping and regrouping tens and hundreds and the composition and decomposition of tens and hundreds. Their purpose is not to determine mastery. Students will display different understandings of how to decompose numbers and how to compute mentally, and their understanding will vary from experience to experience, particularly as they begin to construct their understanding of these concepts.

Use the following assessment techniques throughout this unit. Before a lesson, think about some questions to ask yourself and your students. Be open to and provide time for students' responses and probe their thinking by asking follow-up questions that require them to explain further. As you observe, note students' behavior as well as their conceptual understanding. (For example, some students might exhibit confidence, while others may give up easily.) Whenever possible, record students' responses over time to assess growth in their conceptual understanding.

Observe Individual Students as They Explore Numbers

As students work, observe individuals and ask yourself questions, such as:

Q. Does the student have a sense of the relative magnitude of tens and hundreds?

Students need many opportunities to discuss and experience numbers in context before they develop a sense of their magnitude. Activities such as finding and discussing examples of tens and hundreds in newspapers and magazines or determining the relationship of one number to another (for example, is it larger or smaller? about half? almost the same? close to?) help students develop an understanding of the relative magnitude of numbers.

Q. Is the student able to compose and decompose numbers in many different ways?

Students may not recognize that numbers such as 458 can be decomposed in many ways (such as: 4 hundreds, 5 tens, and 8 ones; 1 hundred, 35 tens, and 8 ones; 45 tens, and 8 ones; or 458 ones). Students need many experiences decomposing numbers similar to the experiences in this unit. Students construct an understanding of composition and decomposition over time.

Q. Does the student regroup ten sets of ten to one set of one hundred? If there are not enough to make another hundred, does the student count the remaining objects by tens and ones?

Some students may not regroup ten sets of ten to one set of one hundred. Some students may count the extra ones as tens or hundreds. (For example, a student might have two sets of one hundred, a set of ten, and 2 ones, and then count them "one hundred, two hundred, three hundred, four hundred, and five hundred.") These students will need more experiences grouping and regrouping. Students construct an understanding of grouping and regrouping over time.

Student Writing

Throughout the unit, ask students to verbalize their thinking, and at times to explain their thinking in writing. During this unit, students write

- Number clues.
- Statements about numbers.
- Strategies for solving problems.
- Number riddles.

Base Ten Activities

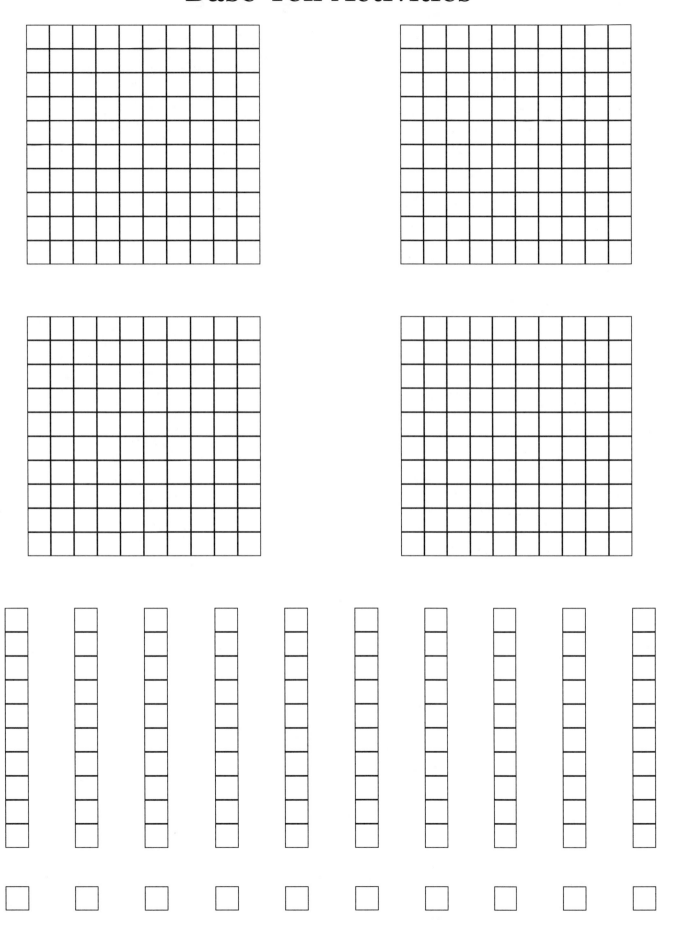

What's the Number?

Students choose a two- or three-digit number and write clues describing the number for another pair to guess. This lesson may take more than one class period.

Team Builder Emphasis

In this lesson, students

- Meet and work with their partner.
- Begin to develop an effective working relationship.

Students add to their understanding that

- Numbers can be used to describe quantities.

Social Emphasis

In this lesson, students

- Listen to each other.
- Share the work.
- Agree on a name and clues.

Students continue to

- Develop group skills.
- Relate the values of fairness, caring, and responsibility to behavior.

Group Size: 2, and then 4

Teacher Materials

- Materials for forming pairs (see Before the Lesson)
- Transparency of "What's the Number?" clue sheet
- Drawing paper
- Marker
- Examples of two- and three-digit numbers from newspapers and magazines

Student Materials

Each pair needs

- Access to a Hundred Chart
- Access to a Two-Hundred Chart
- Drawing paper

Extension Materials

Each student needs

- Examples of two- and three-digit numbers (see Extensions)

Before the Lesson

- Decide how you will form pairs to work together during the unit. (See Forming Groups, p. xiii, for random-grouping suggestions.) Prepare any materials needed.

- Students may need to use a Hundred Chart or a Two-Hundred Chart to help them determine the number described by the clues in the lesson introduction and when they write number clues. Take time to introduce these charts, if students are unfamiliar with them. Ask questions, such as:

> Q. What are some numbers that are closer to 80 than to 100?

> Q. What are some numbers that are greater than 50, but less than 75?

> Q. What are some numbers that have a 2 as one of their digits?

Ask similar questions to help students explore the Two-Hundred Chart.

Notes

Provide time for partners to introduce themselves and to share a few things about themselves.

For example, students might say that they know that 10 tens equals 100, or that 250 is equal to 25 tens.

Encourage students to focus on the information provided in each clue and the range of possible numbers that fit, rather than trying to guess a specific number.

Teacher

Form pairs using the activity you have chosen. Be sure partners know each other's names. Explain that pairs will work together during this unit as the class explores tens and hundreds. First in pairs, then as a class, ask students to discuss what they already know about the relationship of tens and hundreds.

Introduce the lesson by playing What's the Number? State that you are thinking of a two-digit number. One at a time, show the first set of clues on the "What's the Number?" transparency. First in pairs, then as a class, discuss each clue before you show the next one. Ask questions, such as:

Q. What do we know about the number? What numbers might fit this clue? How do you know? Are there any other possibilities?

When you show the fourth clue, ask questions, such as:

Q. What's the number? How do you know?

Q. Do you agree or disagree? Why?

Students

•• ••

•• ••

Play the game again with the second set of clues.

As a class, analyze both sets of clues. Discuss how the first clue in each set eliminates some numbers but leaves the possibility that the number could be within a large range of numbers, that each clue reveals one additional bit of information that narrows the possibilities, and that the number can be guessed when all the clues are revealed.

Explain that pairs will choose a two- or three-digit number to be the name for their pair (for example, the 99ers or the 250s) and then make a table sign with the number on one side and clues about their number on the other side. State that pairs will then use their signs to play What's the Number? with another pair.

Model how to make the table sign by folding a sheet of drawing paper in half lengthwise and writing a two- or three-digit number on one side. With help from the class, write several clues about the number on the other side of the table sign.

Social Emphasis
Develop group skills.

Facilitate a discussion about how students might work together. Ask questions, such as:

Q. What might you and your partner do that will help you work well together?

Notes	Teacher	Students

Notes

Leave the "What's the Number?" transparency on the overhead to show examples of clues.

If pairs are having difficulty working together, help them analyze the situation by posing open-ended questions, such as:

Q. What seems to be causing problems? What might you do to change this?

Q. What have you tried? What else could you try? How might that help?

Teacher

Observe pairs working and, when appropriate, ask questions, such as:

Q. **How are you making sure the clues make sense?**

Q. **How are you and your partner working cooperatively?**

Students

●● In pairs, students

1. Choose a two- or three-digit number to be the name for their pair.

2. Make a table sign with their number on one side and clues that reveal their number on the other side.

Social Emphasis
Relate the values of fairness, caring, and responsibility to behavior.

Teacher

Assign two pairs to work together. Explain that pairs will take turns reading the clues they wrote and guessing each other's number. Suggest that pairs show their clues one at a time. Remind pairs to keep their number a secret until the other pair guesses it. Facilitate a discussion about how pairs might work together. Ask questions, such as:

Q. **What are some things you and your partner can do to work well with another pair?**

Q. **If the other pair's clues do not make sense to you, how could you ask them what they mean without hurting their feelings?**

Students

●● ●●
●● ●●

Teacher

Observe students and, when appropriate, ask questions, such as:

Q. **How are you and your partner showing the other pair that you are listening to their clues?**

Q. **Could the clues describe another number? Why?**

Students

●●

In groups, pairs take turns sharing their clues and guessing another pair's number.

Unit 1   **Exploring Tens and Hundreds**

Notes	Teacher	Students

Have one or two pairs share their clues with the class. Ask questions, such as:

Q. **What does this clue tell us? What numbers fit this clue?**

Q. **What number is this pair describing? How do you know?**

Q. **Could it be another number? Why?**

Q. **What are some other clues that could be written about this number?**

Help students reflect on the lesson by asking questions, such as:

Q. **What did you find out about how to work cooperatively with a partner? How will that help you the next time you work together?**

Q. **Did you have any problems working together? What might you do differently the next time you work together?**

Q. **Was it difficult to agree on a number to use as a name or on clues to write? Why? What did you do?**

Have pairs save their table signs to use each time they work together during the unit.

Show several examples of two- and three-digit numbers from magazine and newspaper headlines and advertisements. Discuss the numbers and post them on the "Numbers in Our World" bulletin board (see the Overview, p. 2). Ask students to help find magazine and newspaper headlines and advertisements at school and at home that show two- and three-digit numbers to post on the "Numbers in Our World" bulletin board.

To help students develop their understanding of number meaning and relationships, have pairs investigate the activities in Extensions For the Next Day before going on to the next lesson.

Mathematical Emphasis
Numbers can be used to describe quantities.

Social Emphasis
Develop group skills.

 **Extensions**

For Pairs That Finish Early

■ Suggest that students get to know their partners better. Encourage them to discuss things such as their favorite books, TV programs, toys, subjects in school, or foods.

For the Next Day

■ Discuss numbers students have collected for the "Numbers in Our World" bulletin board activity (see the Overview, p. 2).

■ Begin the Base Ten Activities described in the Overview, p. 3.

What's the Number?
Clue Sheet

Clues for the first number

1. The number is greater than 20 but less than 50.

2. The number is closer to 20 than to 40.

3. The number is greater than two dozen.

4. The number is one more than half of 50.

Clues for the second number

1. The number is greater than 225 but less than 775.

2. The number is closer to 225 than to 560.

3. The number has the same three digits.

4. If we had this amount in dollars, dimes, and pennies we would have three pennies.

Hundred Chart

1	2	3	4	5	6	7	8	9	10
11	12	13	14	15	16	17	18	19	20
21	22	23	24	25	26	27	28	29	30
31	32	33	34	35	36	37	38	39	40
41	42	43	44	45	46	47	48	49	50
51	52	53	54	55	56	57	58	59	60
61	62	63	64	65	66	67	68	69	70
71	72	73	74	75	76	77	78	79	80
81	82	83	84	85	86	87	88	89	90
91	92	93	94	95	96	97	98	99	100

Two-Hundred Chart

101	102	103	104	105	106	107	108	109	110
111	112	113	114	115	116	117	118	119	120
121	122	123	124	125	126	127	128	129	130
131	132	133	134	135	136	137	138	139	140
141	142	143	144	145	146	147	148	149	150
151	152	153	154	155	156	157	158	159	160
161	162	163	164	165	166	167	168	169	170
171	172	173	174	175	176	177	178	179	180
181	182	183	184	185	186	187	188	189	190
191	192	193	194	195	196	197	198	199	200

Our Classroom

Students choose several two- and three-digit numbers and use those numbers to write statements about things in the classroom. The lesson will take one class period, and is continued in Extensions For the Next Day and in the Extension for Lesson 3.

DAYS AHEAD
1

Mathematical Emphasis

In this lesson, students

- Make reasonable statements about the number of things in the classroom.

Students add to their understanding that

- Numbers can be used to describe quantities.
- Making a reasonable estimate requires gathering and using information.

Social Emphasis

In this lesson, students

- Explain their thinking.
- Listen to the thinking of others.
- Agree on statements.

Students continue to

- Develop group skills.
- Analyze the effect of behavior on others and on the group work.

Group Size: 2

Teacher Materials

- Bulletin board space (see Before the Lesson)
- Four 5″ × 8½″ sheets of tagboard

Student Materials

Each student needs

- Examples of two- and three-digit numbers (see Before the Lesson)

Each pair needs

- 4 sentence strips
- Marker

Extension Materials

Each pair needs

- Sentence strip
- Marker
- Access to self-stick notes
- Access to a calculator
- Paper and a pencil

- Continue with the "Numbers in Our World" bulletin board activity described in the Overview, p. 2.

- Make bulletin board space available for "Our Classroom" statements. You will need enough space to post a series of four sentence strips side by side. (See the illustration on the first page of this lesson for an example of how this might look.)

Notes	Teacher	Students

A cooperative structure such as "Turn to Your Partner" (see p. xii) provides opportunities for all students to be involved in the discussion.

Introduce the lesson by referring to the numbers posted on the "Numbers in Our World" bulletin board. Discuss new numbers that students have posted, then choose one of the numbers (for example, 36) and ask:

Q. Do we have about [36 crayons] in our classroom? How do you know? Do we have about [36 people] in our classroom? How do you know?

Write a sentence such as the following where all can see:

36 could not be the number of books in our classroom, but 36 could be the number of jackets in our classroom.

Ask students if they agree or disagree with this statement and why. Write the following frame sentence where all can see:

___ could not be the number of _____ in our classroom, but ___ could be the number of _____ in our classroom.

Consider asking students to brainstorm things in the room that are easy to count and things that are hard to count. (For example, the number of people in the classroom is easy to count, while the number of sheets of paper in the classroom is hard to count.) This will help students focus on the quantity of things in the classroom.

First in pairs, then as a class, discuss how students might fill in the sentence so that it is a reasonable statement about their classroom.

As a class choose 4 two- or three-digit numbers from the "Numbers in Our World" bulletin board, write the numbers on the 5" × 8½" sheets of tagboard, and post these numbers along the top of the "Our Classroom" bulletin board. (See the illustration on the first page of this lesson.)

Notes	Teacher	Students

| | Explain that pairs will use the four numbers and the frame sentence to write statements on sentence strips about the number of things in the classroom. (Pairs should use different items in the classroom in each of the four sentences.) Explain that pairs will post their statements and then other students will decide if they agree or disagree with the statements. | •• ••

•• •• |

Observe pairs and ask yourself the following questions:

Q. Do students have a reasonable sense of the magnitude of numbers and quantities?

Q. How reasonable are students' estimates of the quantity of specific things in the classroom? For example, do students have a sense of the possible number of books or sheets of paper that might be in the classroom?

Also, note any positive interactions or problems you might discuss when the class reflects on the lesson.

Observe pairs working and, when appropriate, ask questions, such as:

Q. How are you and your partner working together? Do you need to change anything? What might work better?

Q. How do you know your partner is listening to your ideas?

•• In pairs, students

1. Use the frame sentence to write four statements on sentence strips about the number of things in their classroom.

2. Post their sentence strips on the "Our Classroom" bulletin board.

Discuss the importance of disagreeing and giving feedback in a considerate way. Ask students how they might disagree with a pair's statement without hurting their feelings.

Direct students' attention to the posted statements and read several aloud. First in pairs, then as a class, discuss each statement and ask questions, such as:

Q. Do you agree with this statement? Why? If you disagree, how would you change the statement?

Q. What other numbers could we substitute in this statement? Why?

•• ••

•• ••

| **Notes** | **Teacher** | **Students** |

Discuss with the class how pairs might post their self-stick notes on the sentence strips so that the sentences can still be read.

Teacher

Explain that, over the next few days, pairs will have time to read the statements and decide whether they agree or disagree with them. If pairs disagree with a statement they should write their names on a self-stick note and attach it to the statement. State that after a few days the class will discuss the statements and why students agree or disagree with the statements.

Students

●● ●●

●● ●●

Help pairs reflect on the lesson by asking questions, such as:

Q. **What did you like about how you and your partner worked together? Why?**

Q. **What were some problems you had? How did the problems make you feel? How did you solve the problems?**

If appropriate, share some of your observations of the positive interactions and the problems you noted as pairs worked.

Extensions

For Pairs That Finish Early

■ Have pairs choose another number from the "Numbers in Our World" bulletin board and write an additional frame sentence using the new number.

For the Next Day

■ Provide time for pairs to read and agree or disagree with the statements on the "Our Classroom" bulletin board. If pairs disagree with a statement, they should write their names on a self-stick note and attach it to the statement. The class will have time during the Extensions For the Next Day in Lesson 3 to discuss the statements.

■ Continue with the Base Ten Activities described in the Overview, p. 3.

■ Ask pairs to discuss strategies they might use to estimate the number of sheets of paper, crayons, or books in the classroom. Have pairs choose one of the strategies and estimate the number of [crayons] in the classroom. (For example, each pair might count their number of crayons and use a calculator to multiply that number by the number of pairs in the class.) As a class, discuss the results and the strategies used.

Is It Close?

Students spin two spinners, find the sum of the numbers generated by the spinners, and compare the relative magnitude of the sum to other numbers. This lesson may take more than one class period.

DAYS AHEAD
1

Mathematical Emphasis

In this lesson, students

- Add tens and hundreds.
- Determine the relative magnitude of numbers.

Students add to their understanding that

- The relative magnitude of numbers can be described.

Social Emphasis

In this lesson, students

- Share the work.
- Explain their thinking.

Students continue to

- Develop group skills.
- Relate the values of fairness, caring, and responsibility to behavior.

Group Size: 2

Teacher Materials

- 2 overhead spinners (see Before the Lesson)
- Transparency of "Is It Close?" group record sheet

Student Materials

Each pair needs

- 2 spinners (see Before the Lesson)
- Access to a Count by Tens Chart
- "Is It Close?" group record sheet

Extension Materials

- Four 8½″ × 11″ signs (see Before the Lesson)

Each pair needs

- Number card (see Before the Lesson)
- Access to a Count by Tens Chart
- Access to self-stick notes

Before the Lesson

- Make two spinners for each pair and two overhead spinners for yourself using the blackline masters (see "Directions for Making Spinners" for instructions). One spinner will have a face labeled with tens (0–90) and one spinner will have a face labeled with hundreds (100–600). It is helpful if the student spinner labeled 0–90 is a different color from the student spinner labeled 100–600.

- If students have not previously worked with spinners, allow time for free exploration before this lesson.

- For Extensions, prepare a number card for each pair by copying the Number Cards blackline masters and cutting on the dotted lines.

- Also for Extensions, make four 8½″ × 11″ signs labeled as follows: Closer to 250; Closer to 500; Closer to 750; and Closer to 1000.

Notes

Students may need to use a Count by Tens Chart to help them determine the relative magnitude of the numbers discussed. If students are unfamiliar with this chart, take some time to introduce it prior to playing the game.

Some of the sums will belong in more than one box (for example, 610). The "Numbers that do not fit" box on the group record sheet accommodates sums that do not fit in any other boxes (for example, 410).

Teacher

Introduce the lesson by showing the spinners and explaining that pairs will play a game in which they decide whether a number is closer to one number than another.

Explain that pairs will spin the spinners and add the two numbers generated by the spinners. Model this using the overhead spinners and having students add the numbers. Show the "Is It Close?" transparency and have pairs decide in which box to write the sum.

With a student, model playing the game and working cooperatively. As a class, discuss what you and your partner did that helped you work well together. For example, you might want to discuss such things as sharing the spinning of the spinners, together adding the two numbers indicated by the spinners, listening and sharing ideas about where to place the sum, and agreeing in which box to place the sum.

Students

•• ••

•• ••

Notes	Teacher	Students

As you observe students working, ask yourself questions, such as:

Q. How are students handling differences of opinion?

Q. How are students finding the sums?

Q. How are students handling such numbers as 450?

Q. Do students have a sense of the magnitude of a number in relation to other numbers?

If students have trouble cooperating with each other, help them analyze the situation by posing open-ended questions, such as:

Q. How do you feel about how you are playing the game?

Q. What seems to be causing problems?

Q. What could you do about that? How might that help?

Observe pairs working. Ask questions, such as:

Q. How are you finding the sums?

Q. Where would you place the number 200? Why?

Q. Have you placed a number in the "Numbers that do not fit" box? Why?

Q. Have you put any numbers in more than one box? Which numbers? Why did you decide they belong in these boxes?

Q. How are you sharing the work? Is that helping you and your partner work?

Q. How are you helping your partner understand your thinking?

●● In pairs, students

1. Spin the two spinners and find the sum of the two numbers generated.

2. Decide in which box the sum belongs.

3. Record on the group record sheet and prepare to share their thinking.

Mathematical Emphasis

The relative magnitude of numbers can be described.

Encourage students to explain their thinking.

Students may place the same number in different boxes. Accept any placements that students can justify. Use this situation to extend students' thinking about the relative magnitude of numbers.

Show the "Is It Close?" transparency. Have several pairs share one of their sums and the box in which they placed the sum. Check for agreement on the part of the class. Ask students to explain why they agree or disagree. Ask questions, such as:

Q. Could this sum (point to a sum) **fit in another box? Explain.**

Q. Where could a sum of [600] be placed? Why?

Q. Where could a sum of [450] be placed? Why?

●● ●●

●● ●●

Q. How did you decide which numbers to put in the "Numbers that do not fit" box?

Q. How is this lesson similar to or different from other lessons we have done?

•• ••

•• ••

Social Emphasis
Relate the values of fairness, caring, and responsibility to behavior.

Help students reflect on their work together. Facilitate a discussion about responsibility and ask questions, such as:

Q. What does it mean to act responsibly or to take responsibility?

Q. How did you and your partner act responsibly?

Q. What problems did you and your partner have? How might you avoid those problems next time?

To help students develop their understanding of the relative magnitude of numbers, have pairs investigate the activities in Extensions before going on to the next lesson.

Extensions

For Pairs That Finish Early

- Have pairs make up their own categories for sorting the numbers, such as More than 500/Less than 500 or Closer to 500/Closer to 1000, and have pairs re-sort their numbers.

For the Next Day

- In the four corners of the room, hang the signs made before the lesson (Closer to 250; Closer to 500; Closer to 750; Closer to 1000). Distribute a number card to each pair (see Before the Lesson). Ask pairs to read the number, decide in which of the four corners the number belongs, and then stand in that corner of the room. (Pairs might need to use a Count by Tens Chart to help them determine the relative magnitude of their numbers.) Ask pairs to share with the class why they think their number is closer to 250, 500, 750, or 1000.

- Provide time for pairs to read the statements on the "Our Classroom" bulletin board (see Lesson 2). Have pairs write their names on self-stick notes and post them on the statements with which they disagree. As a class, discuss the statements with which students disagree. Facilitate a discussion about how the statements might be changed so that all would agree with them.

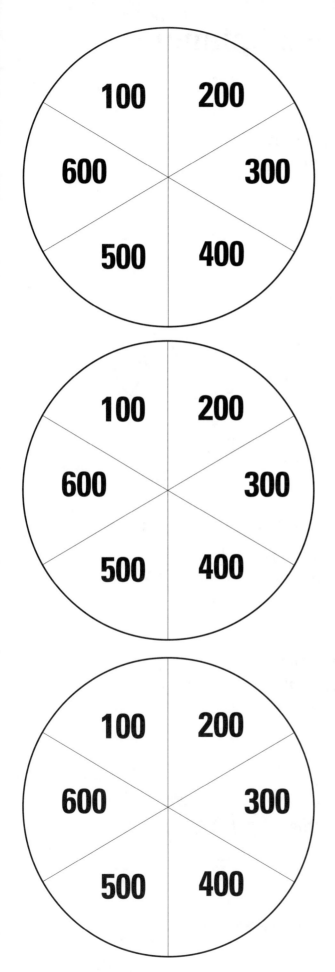

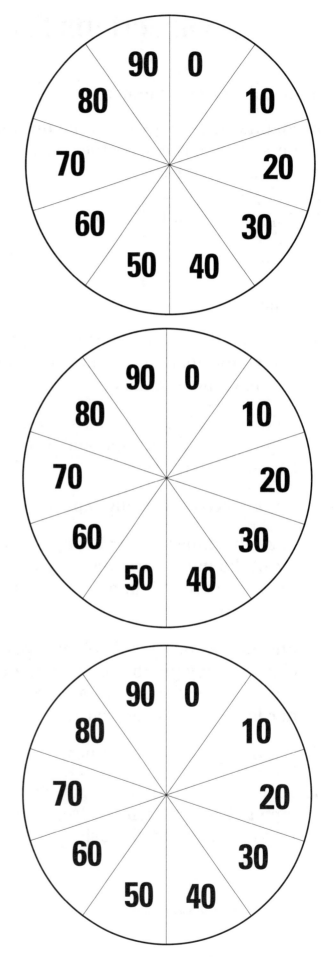

Directions for Making Spinners*

Materials for one spinner

- Spinner face (copy blackline master and cut; copy on a transparency for the overhead spinners)
- 3" × 5" index card
- 3/8" piece of a drinking straw
- paper clip or a bobby pin
- ruler
- tape

Instructions

1. Bend up the outside part of the paper clip as shown (or open up a bobby pin) and use the point to poke a hole in the center of the spinner face.

2. Poke a hole in the center of an index card with the paper clip or bobby pin and draw a line from the center to one corner.

3. Cut a piece of masking tape about 2" long.

4. Poke the paper clip or bobby pin through the center of the index card and tape it on the bottom of the card to hold it in place. (The top of the card has the line.)

5. Put the 3/8" piece of drinking straw on the paper clip or bobby pin that is sticking through the top of the card. It will serve as a washer to keep the spinner face off the index card.

6. Put the spinner face on next.

7. Cover the point of the paper clip with a piece of tape to keep the spinner from spinning off (this step can be omitted if using a bobby pin).

tape

---

* Adapted from *The Math Solution* by Marilyn Burns. (Sausalito, CA: The Math Solution Publications, 1991.)

Is It Close?

Spin the two spinners, add the two numbers, and decide in which box to write the sum. Some of the sums can be written in more than one box.

Less than 200	More than 200 but less than 400

More than 600	Closer to 500 than 400

Numbers that do not fit

Count by Tens Chart

10	20	30	40	50	60	70	80	90	100
110	120	130	140	150	160	170	180	190	200
210	220	230	240	250	260	270	280	290	300
310	320	330	340	350	360	370	380	390	400
410	420	430	440	450	460	470	480	490	500
510	520	530	540	550	560	570	580	590	600
610	620	630	640	650	660	670	680	690	700
710	720	730	740	750	760	770	780	790	800
810	820	830	840	850	860	870	880	890	900
910	920	930	940	950	960	970	980	990	1000

| 130 | 490 |

| 800 | 540 |

| 320 | 70 |

| 940 | 1050 |

230	**460**
780	**610**
280	**210**
990	**720**

One Thousand Dollars

Students mentally compose and decompose numbers as they play a trading game.

DAYS AHEAD
2

Mathematical Emphasis

In this lesson, students

- Regroup ones, tens, and hundreds.

Students add to their understanding that

- Numbers can be composed and decomposed.
- Our place value system is based on an organizational structure of grouping and regrouping.

Social Emphasis

In this lesson, students

- Give help when needed.
- Agree before trading.

Students continue to

- Develop group skills.
- Analyze the effect of behavior on others and on the group work.

Group Size: 4

Teacher Materials

- Transparencies of One Thousand Dollars trading mat and play money (see Before the Lesson)

Student Materials

Each student needs

- One Thousand Dollars trading mat (see Before the Lesson)
- Envelope of play money (see Before the Lesson)

Each group of four needs

- Thousand-dollar play money bill (see Before the Lesson)
- 2 special dice (see Before the Lesson)
- "Pot" (a paper plate)

- For each student, prepare a trading mat by copying the two "Student Trading Mat" blackline masters and taping the two halves together. Each student will also need ten of each of the following denominations of play money: $1, $10, and $100. Copy and cut the bills from the "Student Play Money" blackline masters and put in an envelope for each student. Each group will need a one thousand-dollar bill. The play money will be used in other lessons in the unit.

- Make two dice for each group, one numbered 4 to 9 and one labeled $1, $1, $10, $10, $100, $100. Write the numbers on adhesive dots and place the dots on regular dice, or purchase blank dice at a supply store.

- Make transparencies of the "Overhead Trading Mat" and the "Overhead Play Money" using the blackline masters.

- Familiarize yourself with the game before introducing it to the class. Note possible strategies students might use when they trade bills.

Notes

Note students' sense of the value of money. While some students will have a sense of the value of money, other students may think they could purchase a new automobile for $1000.

Teacher

Combine pairs to form groups of four. First in groups, then as a class, discuss the following question:

Q. What would you do if you had one thousand dollars?

State that groups will play a money-trading game called One Thousand Dollars. Show the "Overhead Trading Mat" transparency and explain the rules:

1. The goal of the game is for the group to have a thousand-dollar bill in their "pot."

2. Each student, in turn, rolls two dice, and takes from his or her envelope the amount of money indicated by the dice. (For example, if a student rolls a 4 and a $100, he or she takes 4 one hundred-dollar bills from his or her envelope.) The student then places this money on his or her trading mat, and reads aloud the total amount on the mat.

3. When a student has 10 ones or 10 tens, he or she must trade them for a bill of the next denomination. All group members must agree that the trade is appropriate. After the trade, the student again reads aloud the total on his or her mat.

Students

Notes	Teacher	Students

4. Whenever a student gets $100, he or she puts the hundred-dollar bill in the "pot."

5. The group keeps track of the amount of money in the "pot." When they have 10 hundred-dollar bills, they trade them for the thousand-dollar bill.

You might want to discuss such things as making sure all group members agree before trades are made and helping each other with trades.

With several students, model playing several rounds of the game. As a class, discuss what you and your group did that helped you work well together and the importance of reading the amount of money on the trading mat.

Mathematical Emphasis

Our place value system is based on an organizational structure of grouping and regrouping.

Observe groups playing the game. Ask questions that help students focus on the mathematics involved, such as:

Q. How much money do you have? How much more money will you need to trade for $100? How do you know?

Q. How did you make that trade?

Q. How many more hundred-dollar bills do you need to add to your "pot" to trade for the thousand-dollar bill? How do you know?

Q. How are you checking that you all agree to a trade?

Social Emphasis

Analyze the effect of behavior on others and on the group work.

If groups are having difficulty working together, ask questions, such as:

Q. What is the problem? What needs to be different?

Q. What have you tried? What else could you try?

In groups, students

1. Take turns playing the game.

2. Agree to each trade and help each other with trades.

Notes	**Teacher**	**Students**

Help the class reflect on the activity by asking questions, such as:

Q. Did your group have the thousand-dollar bill in your "pot" at the end of the game? If not, how much more money would your group need to be able to trade for a thousand-dollar bill? How do you know?

Q. How many ones equal 10? How many tens equal 100? How many hundreds equal 1000?

Q. If I had $450 and wanted to exchange it for all $10 bills, how many $10 bills would I have after the exchange? How do you know?

Q. What did you like about the way your group worked?

Q. What problems did your group have working together? How did you solve them?

Q. Did you ask for help? What did you say? Did you get the help you needed?

Q. Did someone ask you for help? What did you do? How did that make you feel?

Social Emphasis
Develop group skills.

Extensions

For Groups That Finish Early

■ Have groups play the game again, as they will benefit from playing this game many times. Ask questions to help students focus on the mathematics involved.

For the Next Day

■ Have the game available for groups to play when they have free time, or play the game as a class activity.

■ Continue with the Base Ten Activities described in the Overview, p. 3.

■ Facilitate a discussion about the examples of the two- and three-digit numbers posted on the "Numbers in Our World" bulletin board described in the Overview, p. 2.

One Thousand Dollars
Overhead Trading Mat

$100

$10

$1

One Thou

Student

$100	**$1**

sand Dollars
Trading Mat

0	$1

For use on the overhead projector. Make a transparency and cut apart.

$1	$1	$1
$1	$1	$1
$1	$1	$1
$10	$10	$10
$10	$10	$10
$10	$10	$10
$100	$100	$100
$100	$100	$100
$100	$100	$1000

$1	$1
$1	**$1**
$1	**$10**
$10	**$10**

$10	$10
$100	**$100**
$100	**$100**
$100	**$1000**

Bank Teller

Students choose a two- or three-digit number and make that amount using as many different combinations of play money as they can.

DAYS AHEAD
1

Mathematical Emphasis

In this lesson, students

- Compose and decompose numbers.

Students add to their understanding that

- Numbers can be composed and decomposed.
- Our place value system is based on an organizational structure of grouping and regrouping.
- Once a rule to generate a pattern has been identified, the pattern can usually be extended.

Social Emphasis

In this lesson, students

- Explain their thinking.
- Listen to the thinking of others.
- Share the work.

Students continue to

- Develop group skills.
- Relate the values of fairness, caring, and responsibility to behavior.

Group Size: 2

Teacher Materials

- Extra play money (see Before the Lesson)

Student Materials

Each pair needs

- Access to envelope of play money (see Before the Lesson)
- Paper and a pencil

Extension Materials

- Number cards (see Before the Lesson)

Each pair needs

- Paper and a pencil
- "Make It Large" place value mat and number cards (see Before the Lesson)

■ Each pair needs access to at least 20 one-dollar bills, 20 ten-dollar bills, and 10 one-hundred-dollar bills (see blackline master, Lesson 4). Students can combine their bills from the previous lessons.

■ During the lesson, students may explore amounts of money greater than the supply in their envelopes. Have approximately 200 extra one-dollar and ten-dollar bills available for students to use.

■ For Extensions, prepare a place value mat for each pair by copying the two "Make It Large" blackline masters and taping the halves together. Copy and cut apart one set of 10 number cards for each pair and one set for yourself.

Notes	**Teacher**	**Students**

Teacher

Introduce the lesson by telling a story, such as:

I went to the bank yesterday to withdraw $136 dollars from my checking account. I asked for the money in fifties, twenties, fives, and ones but the teller said he did not have any fifties, twenties, or fives. He gave me a hundred-dollar bill, 3 ten-dollar bills, and 6 one-dollar bills.

A cooperative structure such as "Turn to Your Partner" (see p. xii) provides opportunities for all students to be involved in the discussion.

Ask:

Q. What kinds of bills did the teller have?

Q. What other ways could the teller have given me $136 if he had only hundreds, tens, and ones?

Write $136 where all can see and list the different combinations of bills (for example: 136 one-dollar bills; or 13 ten-dollar bills and 6 one-dollar bills).

For example, a pair might choose $149 and make combinations such as:

■ 149 one-dollar bills;
■ 14 ten-dollar bills and 9 one-dollar bills; or
■ 1 hundred-dollar bill, 4 ten-dollar bills, and 9 one-dollar bills.

Explain that pairs will act as a bank teller, choose an amount of money from $50 to $999, and record that amount. Ask pairs to then find and list as many ways as they can to make their amount of money using any combination of hundred-dollar bills, ten-dollar bills, and one-dollar bills.

Notes	**Teacher**	**Students**

Students might mention such things as the importance of sharing the work, listening to their partner, making decisions together, explaining their thinking to their partner, and making sure they both understand each idea.

Facilitate a discussion about how students might work together. Ask questions, such as:

Q. What have you learned about working with a partner that might help you and your partner work well together?

•• ••

•• ••

Pairs might choose to use play money, to draw pictures, or to use mental computation to solve this problem. Pairs may not have enough play money in their envelopes to make all the combinations they might wish to explore. Have a large supply of extra ten-dollar and one-dollar bills available for them to use if needed.

Observe pairs and ask yourself the following questions:

Q. Are students able to decompose a number in many different ways?

Q. Are students beginning to recognize a pattern? If so, are they explaining it to their partner? How?

Q. Do students persevere? Do they try to find many solutions?

Also, note any positive interactions between students or problems you might discuss when the class reflects on the lesson.

Observe pairs working and, when appropriate, ask questions, such as:

Q. What are other possible ways to make your amount of money using hundred-dollar bills, ten-dollar bills, and one-dollar bills?

Q. How do you know your partner understands the different ways to make the amount of money you and your partner have chosen? How are you making sure you understand?

Q. How are you sharing the work? Do you both think that is fair? Why?

•• In pairs, students

1. Agree on a two- or three-digit number and record it.

2. Find many different ways to make that amount of money using hundred-dollar bills, ten-dollar bills, and one-dollar bills and record these combinations.

Notes	**Teacher**	**Students**

Mathematical Emphasis

Numbers can be composed and decomposed.

Ask several pairs to share their findings with the class. Ask questions, such as:

Q. What amount of money did you and your partner choose? What are the different ways to make that amount of money using hundred-dollar bills, ten-dollar bills, and one-dollar bills? Are there other ways? Explain.

Draw the following chart where all can see:

$100s	$10s	$1s

For example, if the amount of money is $250, the chart might look like:

$100s	$10s	$1s
2	5	0
1	15	0
0	25	0
0	15	100

Have a pair share their amount of money and the different ways they made that amount of money. Fill in the chart accordingly. Ask questions, such as:

Q. What do you notice about the different ways to make the amount of money?

Q. What patterns do you notice? Explain.

Q. Do you think you have found all the ways to make the amount of money? Why?

First in pairs, then as a class, discuss questions, such as:

Social Emphasis

Relate the values of fairness, caring, and responsibility to behavior.

Q. How did you act responsibly today? How does that make you feel? How might you be more responsible for your behavior the next time you work with your partner?

If appropriate, share some of your observations of the positive interactions and the problems you noted as pairs worked.

To help students continue to develop an understanding of tens and hundreds and the relative magnitude of two- and three-digit numbers, have pairs investigate the activity in Extensions For the Next Day before going on to the next lesson.

For Pairs That Finish Early

■ Have pairs determine several different ways the amount of money they chose might be represented if they had only fifty-dollar bills, twenty-dollar bills, ten-dollar bills, and one-dollar bills.

For the Next Day

■ With the class, play Make it Large. Ask each pair to use a "Make It Large" place value mat and 10 number cards to try to make the largest three-digit number possible. To play the game:

1. Draw a number card and read the number to the class.

2. Ask pairs to place their matching number card on their place value mat in a way that will help them make the largest number possible. (Pairs may not move the card after they have placed it on their mat.)

3. Continue play until three numbers have been drawn and read to the class. Then discuss the three-digit numbers pairs have made.

Have pairs play the game several times and then write about the strategies they used. Ask several pairs to share their strategies, and discuss them as a class. First in pairs, then as a class, discuss questions, such as:

Q. **What strategies might you use if the goal of the game is to make the smallest number possible?**

Q. **Would you have used the same strategy or a different strategy if the set of number cards included two of each digit 1 through 8 and only one 9?** (Students will need sufficient time to explore and discuss this question.)

Hundreds

Te

Large
Value Mat

ns   **Ones**

4	3	2	1	0
9	8	7	6	5

It's a Riddle!

Students use play money to solve number riddles.

DAYS AHEAD
1

Mathematical Emphasis

In this lesson, students

- Solve riddles.
- Use play money to add and subtract numbers.

Students add to their understanding that

- Numbers can be composed and decomposed.
- Problems may have more than one solution and may be solved in a variety of ways.

Social Emphasis

In this lesson, students

- Share the work.
- Explain their thinking.

Students continue to

- Develop group skills.
- Analyze the effect of behavior on others and on the group work.

Group Size: 2

Teacher Materials

- Sentence strips (see Before the Lesson)
- Play-money transparencies (from Lesson 4)
- Transparency of "It's a Riddle!" group record sheet

Student Materials

Each pair needs

- Access to play money (from Lesson 4)
- "It's a Riddle!" group record sheet

Extension Materials

Each pair needs

- "It's a Riddle! Extension" group record sheet

Each group of four needs

- One Thousand Dollars game materials (see Lesson 4)

What bills might be in my pocket?

I have $110 in my pocket.
I do not have any $100, $50, $20 or $5 bills.

DAYS AHEAD
1

■ Write each line of the following riddles on a sentence strip.

Riddle 1
I have $110.00 in my pocket.
I have only $10 bills.
How many bills do I have in my pocket? What are they?

Riddle 2
I have $103.00 in my pocket.
I do not have any $100, $50, $20, or $5 bills in my pocket.
I have 13 bills in my pocket.
What bills do I have in my pocket?

■ Put 11 ten-dollar play money bills in your pocket for the lesson introduction.

Notes

Provide time for pairs to think about each clue and possible solutions before showing the next clue.

Encourage students to focus on the information provided in each clue and the possible combinations that fit the clues, rather than trying to guess the exact amount.

Teacher

Introduce the lesson by stating that you have $110 in your pocket. Challenge the class to figure out what bills you have. First in pairs, then as a class, have students brainstorm possibilities.

Explain that you have some clues that may help. One at a time, show the sentence strips with the clues for Riddle 1. First in pairs, and then as a class, discuss each clue. Use the transparency play money (from Lesson 4) to illustrate students' responses to questions, such as:

Q. **What information does the clue tell us? What possibilities fit this clue? Are there any other possibilities?**

Q. **How many bills do I have in my pocket? What are they?**

One at a time, show the clues for Riddle 2 and repeat the process. (The solution for Riddle 2 is 10 ten-dollar bills and 3 one-dollar bills.)

Students

•• ••

•• ••

Notes	**Teacher**	**Students**

Notes

The solutions to the riddles on the group record sheet are:

1. 26 ten-dollar bills.

2. There are many solutions, such as:

   12 ten-dollar bills and 4 one-dollar bills; 2 ten-dollar bills and 104 one-dollar bills; or 3 ten-dollar bills and 94 one-dollar bills.

3. The least amount of money: $201 (2 hundred-dollar bills and 1 one-dollar bill).

4. The greatest amount of money: $600 (6 hundred-dollar bills).

   The least amount of money: $402 (4 hundred-dollar bills and 2 one-dollar bills).

   There are many different amounts, such as: $411 (4 hundred-dollar bills, 1 ten-dollar bill, 1 one-dollar bill); $510 (5 hundred-dollar bills, 1 ten-dollar bill); 470 (4 hundred-dollar bills, 1 fifty-dollar bill, 1 twenty-dollar bill).

Teacher

Show the "It's a Riddle!" transparency and explain the directions. Suggest that pairs might use their play money or draw pictures to help them solve the problems. Facilitate a discussion about what might help pairs work together.

Students

•• ••

•• ••

Teacher

Observe pairs working and ask questions, such as:

Q. **How are you sharing the work?**

Q. **How do you know your solution works?**

Q. **How are you explaining your thinking to each other?**

Students

••

In pairs, students discuss and solve the problems on the "It's a Riddle!" group record sheet.

Notes	**Teacher**	**Students**

Have pairs share their solutions. Discuss questions, such as:

Q. How do you know this solution works?

Q. What other solutions might also work? How do you know?

Help students reflect on the lesson by asking questions, such as:

Q. How did the way you and your partner behaved help or hurt the work you did? Do you need to discuss anything with each other? What would you do differently next time?

Social Emphasis

Analyze the effect of behavior on others and on the group work.

Extensions

For Pairs That Finish Early

■ Have pairs complete the "It's a Riddle! Extension" group record sheet.

For the Next Day

■ Have students complete the "It's a Riddle! Extension" group record sheet, if they have not already done so. Discuss the results as a class.

■ Have pairs play One Thousand Dollars (see Lesson 4).

It's a Riddle!

1. I have $260.00 in my pocket.

   I have at least six $10 bills.

   I do not have any $100, $50, $20, $5, or $1 bills.

   How many bills do I have in my pocket?

   What are they?

2. I have $124.00 in my pocket.

   I have at least two $10 bills.

   I do not have any $100, $50, $20, or $5 bills.

   How many bills could I have in my pocket?

   What are they?

3. I have three bills in my pocket.

   I have more than $200.00 but less than $500.00.

   What is the least amount of money in my pocket?

   If I have the least amount of money, what bills
   do I have?

4. I have six bills in my pocket.

   I have more than $400.00 but less than $700.00.

   What is the greatest amount of money I could have,
   and what are the bills?

   What is the least amount of money I could have,
   and what are the bills?

   What other amounts of money could I have,
   and what are the bills?

It's a Riddle!
Extension

1. I ask the bank teller for $251.00.

   She does not have any $100 bills.

   What combinations of bills might she give me?

2. I ask the bank teller for $752.00.

   He does not have any $50 bills.

   What combinations of bills might he give me?

Riddle Book

Students write number riddles and contribute them to a class riddle book.

Mathematical Emphasis

In this lesson, students

- Write number riddles.

Students add to their understanding that

- Numbers can be composed and decomposed.
- Problems may have more than one solution and may be solved in a variety of ways.

Social Emphasis

In this lesson, students

- Explain their thinking.
- Make decisions.
- Include everyone.

Students continue to

- Develop group skills.
- Relate the values of fairness, caring, and responsibility to behavior.

Group Size: 2, and then 4

Teacher Materials

- Riddle sentence strips (from Lesson 6)

Student Materials

Each pair needs

- Envelope of play money (from Lesson 5)
- Paper and a pencil

Extension Materials

Each pair needs

- Paper and a pencil

Each group of four needs

- One Thousand Dollars game materials (from Lesson 4)
- Special die (see Extensions)

Notes	Teacher	Students

Teacher

Introduce the lesson by discussing the activity in the previous lesson. State that pairs will create their own money riddles for other pairs to solve and then the class will make a riddle book.

Direct students' attention to the sentence strips with the two riddles used to introduce the previous lesson. Analyze the riddles as a class. Discuss how the first clue states the total amount of money, that each clue reveals an additional bit of information, and that the riddle can be solved with the clues that are given.

Model writing a number riddle. Write the following where all can see:

I have $301 in my pocket.

Explain that for the riddles today, only hundred-dollar bills, ten-dollar bills, and one-dollar bills will be used. First in pairs, then as a class, discuss the clue and what bills might be in your pocket. Follow one of the students' suggestions, place that number of play money bills on the overhead, and ask:

Q. What might be a good next clue?

Continue to develop the riddle, then ask:

Q. What will be important to think about when writing your riddle?

Q. What have you learned about working cooperatively with a partner that will help you and your partner work well together today?

Notes

A cooperative structure such as "Turn to Your Partner" (see p. xii) provides opportunities for all students to be involved in the discussion.

Pairs will need to decide on an amount of money and a combination of hundred-dollar, ten-dollar, and one-dollar bills that total that amount, then develop their clues.

Notes	Teacher	Students

Notes

Pairs will need their play money to help them write their riddles.

Observe pairs and ask yourself the following questions:

Q. Are students able to decompose a number in many different ways?

Q. Do students exhibit persistence when exploring possible solutions?

Also, note any positive interactions between students or problems you might discuss when the class reflects on the lesson.

Social Emphasis
Relate the values of fairness, caring, and responsibility to behavior.

Teacher

Observe pairs working and, when appropriate, ask questions, such as:

Q. How are you making decisions?

Q. How are you making sure the riddle makes sense?

Have students exchange number riddles with another pair. Ask pairs to solve the riddles, then discuss their solutions with the authors of the riddles, and, if necessary, help each other rewrite the riddles so that they make sense. Facilitate a discussion about how groups might work together. Ask questions, such as:

Q. If the other pair's riddle does not make sense, how might you tell them in a caring and helpful way?

Q. How might you include everyone in this activity?

Observe students and, when appropriate, ask questions, such as:

Q. How do you know the riddle makes sense?

Q. What have you learned about your riddle from the other pair? How did they tell you what they thought? How did that make you feel?

Students

••

In pairs, students write number riddles.

•• ••
•• ••
•• ••
•• ••

In groups, pairs solve each other's riddles and help each other rewrite the riddles, if necessary.

Notes	Teacher	Students

Mathematical Emphasis

Problems may have more than one solution and may be solved in a variety of ways.

Have several pairs share a riddle with the class. First in pairs, then as a class, discuss solutions. Check for agreement or disagreement, and ask questions, such as:

Q. How did you solve this riddle?

Q. Could there be another solution to this riddle? Why?

Q. What are some other clues that could be written about this amount of money?

Help students reflect on the lesson by asking questions, such as:

Q. What was difficult about writing riddles together? Why? What was easy? Why?

Q. How did you help each other? How did you make decisions? Are you happy with how you made decisions or would you do something differently the next time?

Collect the riddles, make them into a riddle book, and put the book in a place accessible to students.

•• ••

•• ••

Extensions

For Pairs That Finish Early

■ Have pairs write a riddle using only fifty-dollar bills, twenty-dollar bills, ten-dollar bills, and one-dollar bills.

For the Next Day

■ Continue with the Base Ten Activities described in the Overview, p. 3.

■ Have groups of four play a different version of One Thousand Dollars (see Lesson 4). Each group will need a special die labeled $1, $1, $1, $10, $10, $10 to go with the die labeled 4 to 9. (The die labeled $1, $1, $10, $10, $100, $100 will not be used in this game.) In this version of One Thousand Dollars, each student starts with $100 and trades backward every time he or she rolls the dice. For example, if a student rolls a 6 and a $10, he or she trades in the hundred-dollar bill for 10 ten-dollar bills and puts 6 ten-dollar bills in the pot, leaving $40 on his or her trading mat. The goal of the game is for the group to have $400 in the pot.

The Crazy ATM

Students design an automatic teller machine that gives unexpected amounts of money.

Transition Emphasis

In this lesson, students

- Develop and solve problems.

Students add to their understanding that

- Once a rule to generate a pattern has been identified, the pattern can usually be extended.
- Numbers can be composed and decomposed.
- Problems may have more than one solution and may be solved in a variety of ways.

Social Emphasis

In this lesson, students

- Explain their thinking.
- Make decisions.
- Share the work.

Students continue to

- Develop group skills.
- Relate the values of fairness, caring, and responsibility to behavior.

Group Size: 2

Teacher Materials

- Transparency of "The Crazy ATM Story" blackline master
- Transparency of "The Crazy ATM" direction sheet

Student Materials

Each pair needs

- Access to envelope of play money (from Lesson 5)
- Paper and a pencil

Extension Materials

Each pair needs

- "The Crazy ATM: Extension" group record sheet

Before the Lesson

■ If students have not had experiences developing number patterns, play games such as What's My Rule? to help students explore number patterns. For example:

1. Explain that you have an In/Out Machine. When you put a number in the In/Out Machine, it follows a secret rule and changes the number.

2. State that if you put 5 in the machine, a 9 will come out. If you put 6 in, a 10 will come out. Draw the following where all can see:

In	Out
5	9
6	10

3. Ask: What will happen if I put in a 7? an 8? a 9? Continue filling in the chart:

In	Out
5	9
6	10
7	?
8	?
9	?

4. Ask students what rule your In/Out Machine is following. Discuss the pattern.

Repeat this activity several times. Then have pairs make their own In/Out Machines and share them with the class.

Notes	**Teacher**	**Students**

Teacher

Introduce the lesson by asking students if they or someone they know has ever used an automatic teller machine (ATM). Ask questions, such as:

Q. What is an automatic teller machine?

Q. How does an automatic teller machine work?

Explain that when you want money from your account, the ATM will give it to you in multiples of either ten or twenty. List multiples of ten and multiples of twenty where all can see. For example:

Notes

Students will not be able to describe technically how an ATM works, but many students will know that you can use an ATM to get money from your bank account.

Students

●● ●●

●● ●●

Multiples of 10	Multiples of 20
10	20
20	40
30	60
40	80
•	•
•	•

Ask questions, such as:

Q. What do you notice about these numbers?

Q. Are any multiples of ten also multiples of twenty? Are any multiples of ten not multiples of twenty? Explain.

Q. Is $267 a multiple of ten? A multiple of twenty? How do you know? Is $410 a multiple of ten? A multiple of twenty? How do you know?

Show the "The Crazy ATM Story" transparency and tell the following story:

> **The other day I heard a news report about an automatic teller machine, an ATM, that went crazy and gave customers more money than they requested. Although the machine did not give the correct amount of money, it did follow a pattern. According to the news report, the first person in line asked for $30.00 and received $60.00. The second person in line asked for $50.00 and received $100.00. The last person in line made a request for money and received $240.00.**

A cooperative structure such as "Turn to Your Partner" (see p. xii) provides opportunities for all students to be involved in the discussion.

First in pairs, then as a class, discuss the following questions:

Q. What did the ATM seem to be doing?

Q. How much money did the first person in line request from the ATM? How much money did the first person receive?

Q. How much money did the second person in line request from the ATM? How much money did the second person receive?

Q. How much money did the last person receive from the ATM? How much money did the last person in line request? How do you know?

Q. If a person requested $40 from the ATM, how much money would the person receive? How do you know?

Q. If a person requested $60, how much money would the person receive? How do you know?

Q. What pattern did the ATM follow? How do you know?

Show "The Crazy ATM" direction sheet transparency and explain that pairs will design their own crazy ATM. Ask pairs to design their machine so that:

1. It gives a different amount of money than requested by the customer.

2. It follows a pattern.

3. It only accepts requests in multiples of ten and gives amounts of money only in multiples of ten.

4. It does not honor requests larger than $500.

Explain that pairs may decide to draw a picture, write a story, or make a list to show how their ATM works. Suggest that pairs show or write about four customers' experiences with their ATM.

Facilitate a discussion about how pairs might work together. Ask questions, such as:

Q. What will be important to think about when designing your ATM?

Q. What have you learned about working with a partner that will help you and your partner work well together?

Social Emphasis
Develop group skills.

Notes	Teacher	Students

Notes

Note the difference between how pairs worked together at the beginning of the unit and how they are working together now. You might discuss these observations when the class reflects on the lesson.

Teacher

Observe pairs working and, when appropriate, ask questions, such as:

Q. **How are you making decisions?**

Q. **What pattern does your ATM follow? Show me how it works.**

Students

••

In pairs, students design a pattern for their ATM and show or write about four customers' experiences.

Mathematical Emphasis

Once a rule to generate a pattern has been identified, the pattern can usually be extended.

Social Emphasis

Relate the values of fairness, caring, and responsibility to behavior.

Have several pairs share their ATM with the class. Ask questions, such as:

Q. **What pattern is this ATM following? How do you know?**

Q. **How much money would I receive if I requested a withdrawal of [$490] from this ATM? How do you know?**

Help students reflect on how they worked with their partner during the unit. Ask questions, such as:

Q. **How did you act in a responsible way?**

Q. **What did you like about the way you and your partner worked?**

Q. **What caused problems? How did you resolve them?**

Q. **How might you work differently the next time you work with a partner?**

If appropriate, share some of your observations of the differences between how pairs worked together at the beginning of the unit and how they work together now.

Give pairs an opportunity to thank each other and to share with each other what they liked about working together.

•• ••

•• ••

For Pairs That Finish Early

Extensions

■ Have pairs explore the pattern on "The Crazy ATM: Extension" group record sheet.

The Crazy ATM Story

The other day I heard a news report about an automatic teller machine, an ATM, that went crazy and gave customers more money than they requested. Although the machine did not give the correct amount of money, it did follow a pattern. According to the news report, the first person in line asked for $30.00 and received $60.00. The second person in line asked for $50.00 and received $100.00. The last person in line made a request for money and received $240.00.

Requested	Received
$30.00	$60.00
$50.00	$100.00
	$240.00

The Crazy ATM
Direction Sheet

Design your ATM so that:

1. It gives a different amount of money than asked for by the customer.

2. It follows a pattern.

3. It only accepts requests for money in multiples of ten and gives amounts of money only in multiples of ten.

4. It will not give out more than $500.00 at one time.

The Crazy ATM
Extension

What would the crazy ATM pattern be if the first person requested $30.00 and received $120.00, the second person requested $50.00 and received $200.00, and the third person requested $60.00 and received $240.00? Write about the pattern.

Mental Computation

Mathematical Development ▰

This unit builds on the place value concepts explored in the previous unit, "Exploring Tens and Hundreds." Informal concrete experiences provide opportunities for students to investigate strategies for computing mentally. Students are encouraged to use, compare, and discuss strategies of their own invention, as well as to explore several specific strategies. The validity and desirability of multiple strategies is emphasized. In addition, students are encouraged to generalize about how numbers can be composed and decomposed, how decomposed numbers relate to each other, and how operations can be carried out in a variety of ways.

Social Development ▰

The social focus of this unit is to provide opportunities for students to analyze how their behavior and the behavior of others affects the group work and interaction and to analyze why it is important to be caring and responsible. The unit fosters group skills such as explaining thinking, sharing the work, using materials responsibly, and making decisions. Open-ended questions help students examine how the underlying values of fairness, caring, and responsibility relate to behavior and to think about the ways their behavior and the behavior of others affect their group work and interaction.

Students should be randomly assigned to pairs that work together throughout the unit. In Lesson 9, two pairs work together as a group of four.

Mathematical Emphasis ▰

Conceptually, experiences in this unit help students construct their understanding that

- Numbers can be composed and decomposed.

- Operations can be carried out in a variety of ways.

- Problems may have more than one solution and may be solved in a variety of ways.

- Once a rule to generate a pattern has been identified, the pattern can usually be extended.

- Making a reasonable estimate requires gathering and using information.

- Questions about our world can be asked, and data about these questions can be collected, organized, and analyzed.

Social Emphasis ▰

Socially, experiences in this unit help students to

- Develop group skills.

- Analyze the effect of behavior on others and on the group work.

- Analyze why it is important to be fair, caring, and responsible.

Lessons

This unit includes ten lessons and an ongoing mental computation activity. The calendar icon indicates some preparation is needed or that an experience is suggested for the students prior to that lesson.

1. What's Your Name?
(page 77)

Introductory team-building lesson that encourages cooperation between partners as they explore patterns.

2. The Hundred Chart
(page 83)

Pattern lesson in which pairs use a Hundred Chart to discover and write about number patterns.

3. Where Will You Land?
(page 87)

Mental computation lesson in which pairs use a Hundred Chart to add and subtract tens and multiples of ten.

4. Every Which Way
(page 93)

Mental computation lesson in which pairs use a Hundred Chart to write addition and subtraction number sentences.

5. Friendly Numbers
(page 99)

Mental computation lesson in which pairs add compatible numbers that total ten and one hundred.

6. Money!
(page 105)

Mental computation and pattern lesson in which pairs add and subtract the value of coins.

7. What's in My Pocket?
(page 115)

Problem-solving lesson in which pairs solve and write number riddles.

8. Roll the Difference
(page 121)

Subtraction game in which pairs subtract numbers from multiples of one hundred and look for number patterns.

9. Shake, Rattle, and Toss
(page 129)

Probability lesson in which groups of four predict the outcome of an event and mentally add a series of numbers.

10. Mental Math!
(page 135)

Transition lesson in which pairs write problems that can be solved using mental computation and then reflect on their work together.

Mental Computation Activity

This ongoing mental computation activity provides opportunities for students to compute mentally, to explain their thinking, and to try others' strategies. Before each lesson, write an addition or subtraction problem where all can see. Ask students to solve the problem mentally, then to explain their solution and strategy to their partner. Have several students explain their strategies to the class. Choose one of the strategies and have students use it to solve a similar problem mentally. First in pairs, and then as a class, discuss the appropriateness of the strategy for solving the problem and ideas for alternative strategies. (At the beginning of the unit, you might use problems with two-digit numbers, such as 39 + 42 or 84 – 52, and then move to problems with three-digit numbers as the unit progresses.)

Materials ▬▬▬▬▬▬▬▬▬▬▬▬▬▬▬▬▬▬▬▬▬▬▬▬▬▬▬▬

The materials needed for the unit are listed below. The first page of each lesson lists the materials specific to that lesson. All blackline masters for transparencies and group record sheets are included at the end of each lesson. These and many other materials are available in the *Number Power* Package for Grade 3.

Throughout the unit, you will need access to an overhead projector, and students will need access to supplies such as calculators, scissors, crayons, rulers, glue sticks, paper, and pencils. If possible, each group should have a container with these supplies available for their use at their discretion. The Hundred Chart blackline master is located at the end of Lesson 1 in Unit 1 and the Count by Tens Chart blackline masters is located at the end of Lesson 3 in Unit 1. Use these blackline masters to make copies and transparencies for lessons in Units 1, 2, and 3.

Teacher Materials

- Materials for forming pairs (Lesson 1)
- Transparency of 10 by 10 Grid (Lesson 1)
- Transparency of a Hundred Chart (Lessons 2, 3, 4, and 5)
- Transparency of "Where Will You Land?" group record sheet (Lesson 3)
- Transparency of "Every Which Way" group record sheet (Lesson 4)
- Transparencies of coins (Lessons 6 and 7)
- Transparency of "Money!" group record sheet (Lesson 6)
- Sentence strips (Lesson 7)
- 3 dimes, 2 nickels, and a quarter (Lesson 7)
- Transparency of "What's in My Pocket?" group record sheet (Lesson 7)
- Overhead spinner (Lesson 8)
- Transparency of "Roll the Difference" group record sheet (Lesson 8)
- Transparency of "Number Sentences" group record sheet (Lesson 8)
- Penny and paper cup (Lesson 9)
- Transparency of "Shake, Rattle, and Toss" direction sheet (Lesson 9)

Student Materials

Each pair needs

- 10 by 10 Grid (Lessons 1 and 2)
- Hundred Chart (Lessons 2, 3, 4, and 5)
- "Where Will You Land?" group record sheet (Lesson 3)
- "Every Which Way" group record sheet (Lesson 4)
- Baggie of coins (Lessons 6 and 7)
- "Money!" group record sheet (Lesson 6)

Student Materials *(continued)*

- "What's in My Pocket?" group record sheet (Lesson 7)
- Special die and spinner (Lesson 8)
- "Roll the Difference" group record sheet (Lesson 8)
- Calculator (Lesson 8)
- "Number Sentences" group record sheet (Lesson 8)

Each group of four needs

- Penny and paper cup (Lesson 9)
- "Shake, Rattle, and Toss" direction sheet (Lesson 9)
- Calculator (Lesson 9)

Extension Materials

- Transparency of "Money! Extension" blackline master (Lesson 6)
- Box to hold index cards (Lesson 10)

Each student needs

- Hundred Chart (Lesson 2)
- Letter-size envelope (Lesson 2)

Each pair needs

- Hundred Chart (Lessons 1 and 4)
- Count by Tens chart (Lessons 2 and 4)
- 10 by 10 Grid (Lesson 3)
- "Friendly Numbers: Extension" group record sheet (Lesson 5)
- Index cards (Lessons 5 and 10)
- Baggie of coins (Lesson 6)
- Special die and spinner (Lesson 8)
- "Roll the Difference" group record sheet (Lesson 8)
- Calculator (Lesson 8)

Each group of four needs

- Lima bean painted on one side, or another two-sided counter (Lesson 9)

Teaching Hints

- Review each lesson before introducing it. Think about the open-ended questions you might ask to extend or probe students' thinking. Decide which Extensions to have ready when pairs finish early.

- Provide time for students to freely explore materials that are unfamiliar or infrequently used before students use them in a lesson.

- Lead discussions that encourage students to think of ways to share materials and to use them responsibly. For example, in Lesson 6, students might discuss how to use the coins in a responsible and fair way.

- During this unit, students have many opportunities to explain their strategies for computing. Because students often develop complex strategies for computing, their explanations may be lengthy. Encourage students to ask each other questions when they do not understand an explanation. Provide time for students to try other students' strategies. Ask students to add or subtract a second set of numbers using the strategy they have heard.

Assessment Techniques

These informal techniques will help you assess your students' understanding of the composition and decomposition of numbers, how decomposed numbers relate to one another, and how operations can be carried out in a variety of ways. Their purpose is not to determine mastery. Students will display different understandings of how to decompose numbers and how to compute mentally, and their understanding will vary from experience to experience, particularly as they are constructing these concepts.

Use the following assessment techniques throughout this unit. Before a lesson, prepare some questions to ask yourself and your students. Be open to the responses of the students, provide time for students to think, and then probe their thinking by asking follow-up questions that require them to explain further.

Listen to Each Student's Strategies for Computing Mentally

Throughout the unit, listen to individual students as they explain their strategies for computing mentally, and ask yourself questions, such as:

> Q. **Does the student use different mental computation strategies when appropriate?** (Such strategies might include adding compatible numbers, decomposing numbers, doubling and halving numbers, or strategies that students invent.)

> Q. **Can the student compute by decomposing numbers?** (For example, when adding 72 and 84 mentally, can the student decompose 72 to $70 + 2$ and 84 to $80 + 4$ and then add $70 + 80$ and $2 + 4$?)

> Q. **With subtraction problems, such as $800 - 199 = 601$, can the student reason that 199 is almost 200 and $800 - 200 = 600$, so $800 - 199 = 601$?**

Some students may not demonstrate flexibility when computing mentally. Some students may have memorized the standard algorithm for addition and subtraction and use that method to the exclusion of all others. Students need many opportunities to invent their own strategies for computing mentally and to discuss and try other strategies.

Student Writing

Throughout the unit, ask students to verbalize their thinking, and at times to explain their thinking in writing. During this unit, students write

- About patterns they discover on the Hundred Chart.
- Number riddles.
- Problems that can be solved using mental computation strategies.

What's Your Name?

Students share information about their names, find letters their names have in common, use these letters to create a name for their pair, and develop a pattern using this name. This lesson may take more than one class period.

Team Builder Emphasis

In this lesson, students

- Sort letters.
- Develop a pattern.
- Develop a sense of identity as a pair.
- Begin to develop an effective working relationship.

Students add to their understanding that

- Once a rule to generate a pattern has been identified, the pattern can usually be extended.

Social Emphasis

In this lesson, students

- Agree on a name for their pair.
- Make decisions.

Students continue to

- Develop group skills.

Group Size: 2

Teacher Materials

- Materials for forming pairs (see Before the Lesson)
- Transparency of 10 by 10 Grid

Student Materials

Each pair needs

- Paper and a pencil
- 10 by 10 Grid
- Crayons or markers

Extension Materials

Each pair needs

- Hundred Chart

- Decide how you will form pairs to work together during the unit. (See Forming Groups, p. xiii, for random-grouping suggestions.) Prepare any materials needed.

- Have students ask their families or guardians for information about their names, such as how they were named, what their name means, or famous people who have their name.

Notes	Teacher	Students

Teacher

Form pairs using the activity you have chosen. Explain that these pairs will work together during this unit as the class explores ways to add and subtract mentally.

Explain that today pairs will have an opportunity to find out more about each other. Discuss the importance of knowing each other's name and how it makes people feel when others know and use their names. Share your full name and something about it, such as how you were named, why you like your name, or a nickname you have.

Explain that students will take turns telling each other their full names and something they would like to share about their names, such as how they got their names or what they like to be called. Ask pairs to find letters their names have in common and use these letters to create a name for their pair. Explain that pairs need not use all their letters in common for their pair name and that the name they choose does not need to be a real word.

Social Emphasis
Develop group skills.

Model the activity with a student, and ask questions, such as:

Q. What did you notice about how we shared the work? What worked? What didn't work?

Q. What did you notice about how we made decisions? What worked? What didn't work?

Q. What might help you and your partner work together?

Students

•• ••

•• ••

Notes	**Teacher**	**Students**

Have an activity ready for pairs that finish early. See Extensions (p. 80) for suggestions.

Observe pairs working and, when appropriate, ask questions, such as:

Q. **How are you and your partner working together?**

Q. **What strategies are you using to find the letters your names have in common?**

Q. **How do you know you have found all the letters your names have in common?**

Q. **What choices do you have for the name for your pair? How will you decide?**

●● In pairs, students

1. Tell each other their names and something about their names.

2. Find letters their names have in common.

3. Create a name for their pair using the letters their names have in common.

Have pairs share their pair names. Ask questions, such as:

Q. **How did you find the letters you had in common?**

Q. **What were some of your choices for a name for your pair?**

Q. **How did you decide on a name?**

●● ●●

●● ●●

You might wish to do this activity in a second class period.

For example, if a pair's name is ROAMIN, their grid would look like:

Show the 10 by 10 Grid transparency. Ask pairs to write their pair name on the grid by writing one letter in each square, repeating their name over and over until all squares are filled. Have pairs then color in each square with the first letter of their pair name and discuss the result.

Notes	**Teacher**	**Students**
	Observe pairs and, when appropriate, ask questions, such as:	•• In pairs, students
	Q. **What do you notice when you look at your grid?**	1. Fill in a 10 by 10 Grid with their pair name.
		2. Color in each square that has the first letter of their pair name.
		3. Discuss what they notice about the result.

	Have pairs show their grids to the class. Ask questions, such as:	•• ••
Mathematical Emphasis	Q. **What do you notice about this pair's grid?** (Point to grid.) **How is it similar to** [different from] **this pair's grid?** (Point to another grid.)	•• ••
Once a rule to generate a pattern has been identified, the pattern can usually be extended.	Q. **If your grid was a 10 by 13 grid, would your pattern change? Why do you think that?**	
	Q. **What did you find out about your partner?**	
	Q. **What was something your partner did that helped you work well today?**	
	Q. **How did you make decisions?**	
	Save pairs' grids for the next lesson, "The Hundred Chart."	

Extensions

For Pairs That Finish Early

- Have pairs share information with each other about other family members' names.

- Give pairs a Hundred Chart and have them discuss what they notice about the chart and any number patterns they see.

For the Next Day

- Continue with the next lesson, "The Hundred Chart."

10 by 10 Grid

The Hundred Chart

Students look for number patterns on a Hundred Chart, write about the patterns they discover, and share their findings with the class.

Mathematical Emphasis

In this lesson, students

- Explore number patterns.
- Write about patterns.

Students add to their understanding that

- Once a rule to generate a pattern has been identified, the pattern can usually be extended.

Social Emphasis

In this lesson, students

- Explain their thinking.
- Share the work.

Students continue to

- Develop group skills.

Group Size: 2

Teacher Materials

- Transparency of a Hundred Chart (see Unit 1, Lesson 1)
- Marker

Student Materials

Each pair needs

- 10 by 10 Grid (from Lesson 1)
- Hundred Chart (see Unit 1, Lesson 1)
- Paper and a pencil

Extension Materials

Each pair needs

- Count by Tens Chart (see Unit 1, Lesson 3)

Each student needs

- Hundred Chart (see Unit 1, Lesson 1)
- Letter-size envelope
- Scissors

Notes	Teacher	Students

Introduce the lesson by showing the Hundred Chart transparency and asking:

Q. How is the Hundred Chart similar to or different from the grid with your pair name?

●● ●●

●● ●●

Explain that during the next several lessons pairs will explore number patterns on the Hundred Chart and use the number patterns to help them compute mentally.

For example, the pair from the previous lesson would find this pattern using the name for their pair, ROAMIN:

■	O	A	M	I	N	■	O	A	M
I	N	■	O	A	M	I	N	■	O
A	M	I	N	■	O	A	M	I	N
■	O	A	M	I	N	■	O	A	M
I	N	■	O	A	M	I	N	■	O
A	M	I	N	■	O	A	M	I	N
■	O	A	M	I	N	■	O	A	M
I	N	■	O	A	M	I	N	■	O
A	M	I	N	■	O	A	M	I	N
■	O	A	M	I	N	■	O	A	M

①	2	3	4	5	6	⑦	8	9	10
11	12	⑬	14	15	16	17	18	⑲	20
21	22	23	24	㉕	26	27	28	29	30
㉛	32	33	34	35	36	㊲	38	39	40
41	42	㊸	44	45	46	47	48	㊾	50
51	52	53	54	(55)	56	57	58	59	60
(61)	62	63	64	65	66	(67)	68	69	70
71	72	(73)	74	75	76	77	78	(79)	80
81	82	83	84	(85)	86	87	88	89	90
(91)	92	93	94	95	96	(97)	98	99	100

Explain that pairs will translate the pattern from their grid (from Lesson 1) to a Hundred Chart by circling numbers in the same position as those squares colored in on their grid. Ask pairs to then look at their Hundred Chart and discuss the patterns they see. Show the Hundred Chart transparency and model how to translate a pattern from a grid.

Observe pairs and ask questions, such as:

Q. What do you notice about the pattern on your Hundred Chart?

Q. Think about how you are working. How are you sharing the work? How are you making sure you are being accurate?

●● In pairs, students

1. Translate the pattern from their grid to a Hundred Chart.
2. Discuss the patterns they see.

Notes	Teacher	Students
	Have several pairs share their number patterns with the class. Ask questions, such as:	•• •• •• ••
	Q. **What do you notice about this pattern?**	
	Q. **What similarities and differences do you notice about these patterns?** (Show two patterns.)	
	Ask pairs to find other number patterns on their Hundred Chart, to explain them to each other, and then to write about the patterns they discovered. Model writing statements by asking pairs to suggest one or two statements, and then writing them where all can see.	
	Observe pairs working and, when appropriate, ask questions, such as:	•• In pairs, students
	Q. **What other patterns do you see?**	1. Find number patterns on a Hundred Chart and explain them to each other.
	Q. **How would you describe one of the patterns?**	
	Q. **How are you making sure you understand each other's ideas?**	2. Write about the patterns they discovered.
Mathematical Emphasis Once a rule to generate a pattern has been identified, the pattern can usually be extended.	Ask several pairs to share the patterns they discovered. Have pairs circle their patterns on the Hundred Chart transparency and discuss the patterns with the class.	•• •• •• ••

Social Emphasis
Develop group skills.

Help pairs reflect on their work. Ask questions, such as:

Q. **How is this lesson like the previous lesson?**

Q. **How would you describe how your pair worked together?**

Q. **What helped you work well? What problems did you have?**

Q. **How did your partner help you? How did you help your partner?**

Q. **Did it help you to have your partner explain his or her thinking? How?**

Extensions

For Pairs That Finish Early

- Give each pair a Count by Tens Chart. Have them discuss similarities and differences between the Hundred Chart and the Count by Tens Chart. Ask them to find patterns on the Count by Tens Chart.

For the Next Day

- Give each student a Hundred Chart, an envelope, and a pair of scissors. Have each student make a "Hundred Chart Puzzle" by cutting the Hundred Chart into 5 to 10 pieces, writing their names on the back of each piece, and putting the pieces into the envelope. Remind students to cut their puzzle pieces so each square is intact; for example

Have partners switch "Hundred Chart Puzzles" and reassemble.

- Continue with the next lesson, "Where Will You Land?"

Where Will You Land?

Students mentally add and subtract using a system of arrows to move from one number to another on a Hundred Chart. This lesson may take more than one class period.

Mathematical Emphasis

In this lesson, students

- Visualize adding and subtracting numbers on a Hundred Chart.

Students add to their understanding that

- Numbers can be composed and decomposed.
- Operations can be carried out in a variety of ways.
- Problems may have more than one solution and may be solved in a variety of ways.

Social Emphasis

In this lesson, students

- Explain their thinking.
- Share the work.

Students continue to

- Develop group skills.
- Analyze the effect of behavior on others and on the group work.

Group Size: 2

Teacher Materials

- Transparency of a Hundred Chart (see Unit 1, Lesson 1)
- Hundred Chart for each pair (see Unit 1, Lesson 1)
- "Where Will You Land?" group record sheet for each pair
- Transparency of "Where Will You Land?" group record sheet

Extension Materials

Each pair needs

- Paper and a pencil
- 10 by 10 Grid (see Lesson 1)

Notes	Teacher	Students

Show the Hundred Chart transparency. Introduce the lesson by having pairs, then the class, discuss what they discovered about the Hundred Chart during the previous lesson. Ask questions, such as:

•• ••
•• ••

Q. What did you discover about the Hundred Chart in the previous lesson?

Q. What patterns did you discover?

Having students "see" the chart in their minds provides them with another tool for mental computation. For example, when students add 19 + 21, they might visualize moving 2 down and 1 to the right of 19. Increase students' ability to visualize by frequently having them close their eyes and picture the Hundred Chart.

Ask students to look at the Hundred Chart transparency to get a picture of it in their minds. After a minute or less, have students close their eyes and answer questions, such as:

Q. What number is in the square just below 30? [40] Below 1? [11]

Q. What number is in the square to the left of 46? [45] To the right of 91? [92]

Continue asking similar questions, having students open their eyes and check the chart after each question. Do this until students are able to visualize the chart comfortably.

An arrow pointing down (↓) means move down one square, pointing up (↑) means move up one square. An arrow pointing to the left (←) means move to the left one square, pointing to the right (→) means move to the right one square. An arrow pointing diagonally down and to the right (↘) means move diagonally down and to the right one square. An arrow pointing diagonally down and to the left (↙) means move diagonally down and to the left one square.

State that today students will explore an arrow system for moving from one number to another on the Hundred Chart. Write 6→ where all can see. Point to 6 on the Hundred Chart transparency. Ask where you will land if you move one square to the right (7). Ask what is meant by 6→ (start at 6 and move one square to the right).

First in pairs, then as a class, discuss the following questions:

•• ••
•• ••

Q. What might 6⇉ mean?

Q. What might 6↓↓ mean?

Q. What do you think 6↘ means?

Q. What do you think 6↙ means?

Notes	Teacher	Students

An arrow pointing diagonally up and to the right (↗) means move diagonally up and to the right one square, pointing diagonally up and to the left (↖) means move diagonally up and to the left one square.

Distribute a Hundred Chart to pairs. Write the following where all can see:

24↑↑←

Have students look at their Hundred Charts. Ask:

Q. If we follow the arrows, where do we land? [3]

Write the following where all can see:

12↓↓⇉

Have students look at their Hundred Charts, and ask:

Q. If we follow the arrows, where do we land? [34]

Continue asking similar questions until students are able to use arrows to move comfortably around the chart.

Show the Hundred Chart transparency and ask:

There are many solutions, such as

16↓↓⇉
16→↓↓→
16↘↘

Q. Using arrows, how can you get from 16 to 38? Is there any other way?

Q. How can you get from 16 to 38 with the fewest possible moves? Can you find a way that takes five moves?

Do several similar problems.

You may want to do this segment of the lesson on the following day.

Hand out a "Where Will You Land?" group record sheet to each pair. Show the "Where Will You Land?" transparency and discuss the directions. Explain that pairs will find solutions to the problems, making sure they both understand and agree on their solutions.

Ask questions, such as:

Social Emphasis
Relate the values of fairness, caring, and responsibility to behavior.

Q. What problems might pairs have working together? What could be done to solve those problems? How is that fair (or caring or responsible)?

Notes	Teacher	Students

Teacher:

Q. How might you and your partner share the work? How is that fair?

Q. What are some ways to make sure you both understand without hurting each other's feelings?

Students:

•• ••

•• ••

Teacher:

Observe pairs and, when appropriate, ask questions, such as:

Q. What might be another solution to the problem? Why do you think that?

Q. How can you show me that your strategy for this problem works?

Q. How are you making sure you understand each other's thinking?

Students:

••

In pairs, students solve the problems on the "Where Will You Land?" group record sheet.

Notes:

Mathematical Emphasis

Problems may have more than one solution and may be solved in a variety of ways.

Social Emphasis

Analyze the effect of behavior on others and on the group work.

Teacher:

As a class, reflect on the lesson. Discuss students' solutions to the problems on the "Where Will You Land?" group record sheet. Ask questions, such as:

Q. What are some strategies for getting from 25 to 50? What might be the fewest number of moves?

Q. What are some strategies for getting from 15 to 100? How do you know that your strategy works?

Q. How do you think the arrow system might help you with addition and subtraction?

Q. What did you like about the way you and your partner worked together? Why? What might you do the same or differently next time you work together?

Q. Did you and your partner explain your thinking to each other? If so, did it help your work? How?

Students:

•• ••

•• ••

**For Pairs That
Finish Early**

- Have pairs write problems using the arrow system. (For example, "What's the shortest way to get from 30 to 45?") Have pairs share their problems with another pair and solve them.

**For the
Next Day**

- Give each pair a 10 by 10 Grid. Call out a number from 1 to 100 and have pairs locate the square in which the number belongs and write the number in the square. Have pairs discuss how they decided where to write the number. Repeat the process until most of the grid is filled in. Then have pairs complete their grid to make a Hundred Chart.

- Continue with the next lesson, "Every Which Way."

Where Will You Land?

If you follow these arrows, where will you land?

38 ↘ → _____   51 ⇉↑ _____

76↑↑↑ _____   90↓⇇ _____

9↓⇇ _____   44←↖↖ _____

Use arrows to show the following:

At least two ways to go from 25 to 50.

How to go from 91 to 59 using the fewest moves.

At least two ways to go from 69 to 41.

How to go from 2 to 92 in twelve moves.

At least two ways to go from 15 to 100.

Every Which Way

Students write addition and subtraction number sentences for moving from one number to another on a Hundred Chart.

Mathematical Emphasis

In this lesson, students

- Visualize adding and subtracting numbers on a Hundred Chart.
- Write number sentences.

Students add to their understanding that

- Numbers can be composed and decomposed.
- Operations can be carried out in a variety of ways.
- Problems may have more than one solution and may be solved in a variety of ways.

Social Emphasis

In this lesson, students

- Explain their thinking.
- Help each other.
- Share the work.

Students continue to

- Develop group skills.
- Analyze the effect of behavior on others and on the group work.

Group Size: 2

Teacher Materials

- Transparency of a Hundred Chart (see Unit 1, Lesson 1)
- Transparency of "Every Which Way" group record sheet

Student Materials

Each pair needs

- Paper and a pencil
- Hundred Chart (see Unit 1, Lesson 1)
- "Every Which Way" group record sheet

Extension Materials

Each pair needs

- Hundred Chart (see Unit 1, Lesson 1)
- Paper and a pencil
- Count by Tens Chart (see Unit 1, Lesson 3)

Notes	**Teacher**	**Students**

Teacher

Show the Hundred Chart transparency and review the arrow system discussed in the previous lesson. First in pairs, and then as a class, discuss questions, such as:

Q. How can you get from 15 to 47?

Have several pairs share their solutions on the Hundred Chart transparency. Ask questions, such as:

Q. What other solutions are there?

Q. Do you and your partner agree or disagree with this solution? Why?

Write 28↓↓ where all can see. Ask:

Q. What happens to 28 when you move two squares down? (You add 20.)

Q. What are some number sentences that show this? ($28 + 10 = 38$ and $38 + 10 = 48$, or $28 + 20 = 48$)

Write 45↑ where all can see. Ask:

Q. What happens to 45 when you move up one square? (You subtract 10.)

Q. What is a number sentence that shows this? ($45 - 10 = 35$)

Write several more problems, such as those below, and ask pairs to find number sentence solutions.

82↑↑

45 ⇉↓

68 ↘↙

Notes

Students might find a number of solutions, such as:

15↓↓↓⇉

15↘↘↓

15⇉↓↓↓

For example, 82↑↑ could be
$82 - 10 = 72$ and
$72 - 10 = 62$, or
$82 - 20 = 62$.

45⇉↓ could be
$45 + 3 + 10 = 58$,
$45 + 13 = 58$,
or $45 + 1 + 1 + 1 + 10 = 58$.

Notes	Teacher	Students

Teacher

Observe pairs as they work and ask questions such as:

Q. **Show me why you think your number sentence means the same as 82 ↑↑. Is there another way to write this?**

Q. **How might I write 28 – 20 = 8 using the arrow system?**

Students

●●

In pairs, students write number sentences for arrow sentences.

Teacher

As pairs share their number sentences, write them where all can see. Ask students to demonstrate why their solutions work.

Show the "Every Which Way" transparency. Explain that pairs will use arrows to find different ways to move from one number to another on the Hundred Chart and then write number sentence solutions.

Facilitate a discussion about how pairs might work. Ask questions, such as:

Q. **How might you help each other solve the problems?**

Q. **How does it help you if your partner explains his or her ideas?**

Q. **How might you ask your partner to explain his or her thinking?**

Notes

Social Emphasis
Develop group skills.

Students

●● ●●

●● ●●

Notes

Observe students and informally assess how they solve problems. Ask yourself questions, such as:

Q. Do students see more than one solution to a problem?

Q. Can students write an equation that reflects their solution?

Q. How do students explain their computational strategy?

Teacher

Observe pairs working and, when appropriate, ask questions, such as:

Q. **Show me your solution. Why do you think this solution works?**

Q. **What might be another solution to the problem? Why do you think that?**

Students

●●

In pairs, students discuss and find solutions to the problems on the "Every Which Way" group record sheet.

Notes	**Teacher**	**Students**

Teacher

As a class, discuss pairs' solutions. Ask questions, such as:

•• ••

•• ••

Q. What solutions did you find for [43] to [23]? What number sentence did you write for this problem? Did any pair write a different number sentence?

Ask students to close their eyes again. Ask questions, such as:

Q. Start at 11. How would you get to 24? Is there another way?

Q. Open your eyes and look at your record sheet. What number sentence did you write for this problem? Did any pair write a different number sentence?

Q. Turn to your partner and discuss what happens when you add 10 to or subtract 10 from any two-digit number? What happens when you add 11 to or subtract 11 from any two-digit number?

Q. Why was it helpful to explain your thinking to your partner?

Q. How did your partner help you with this activity? How did you help your partner?

To provide opportunities for students to continue to explore number patterns and to add and subtract mentally, have pairs investigate the activities in Extensions before going on to the next lesson.

Notes

Mathematical Emphasis
Problems may have more than one solution and may be solved in a variety of ways.

Social Emphasis
Analyze the effect of behavior on others and on the group work.

Extensions

For Pairs That Finish Early

■ Give pairs a Hundred Chart. Ask them to pick one number in the first row and circle all the numbers that are on a diagonal to that number (for example, 1, 12, 23, 34, 45, and so on). Have the pairs write about any patterns they see.

For the Next Day

■ Have pairs repeat activities similar to those on the "Where Will You Land?" and "Every Which Way" group record sheets using a Count by Tens Chart. Ask pairs how the Count by Tens Chart and Hundred Chart differ from each other and how they are alike. (This Extension may take several days.)

Every Which Way

Use the Hundred Chart to find several ways to get from the first number to the second number. Record your methods using number sentences.

16 to 36

50 to 95

43 to 23

11 to 24

82 to 71

Show ways you could solve 100 – 78 using the arrow system.

Show ways you could solve 48 + 27 using the arrow system.

Friendly Numbers

Students use a Hundred Chart to find pairs of numbers that add to one hundred and then explore the patterns of these compatible, or "friendly," number pairs. This lesson may take more than one class period.

Mathematical Emphasis

In this lesson, students

- Find "friendly" numbers that add to one hundred.
- Explore number patterns.

Students add to their understanding that

- Numbers can be composed and decomposed.
- Once a rule to generate a pattern has been identified, the pattern can usually be extended.
- Operations can be carried out in a variety of ways.

Social Emphasis

In this lesson, students

- Help each other.
- Listen to others.
- Explain their thinking.

Students continue to

- Develop group skills.
- Analyze why it is important to be fair, caring, and responsible.

Group Size: 2

Teacher Materials

- Transparency of a Hundred Chart (see Unit 1, Lesson 1)
- Colored markers

Student Materials

Each pair needs

- Hundred Chart (see Unit 1, Lesson 1)
- Crayons
- Paper and a pencil

Extension Materials

Each pair needs

- "Friendly Numbers: Extension" group record sheet
- 10 index cards

•• ••
•• ••

This lesson provides opportunities for students to think about their strategies for adding a series of numbers and to hear and try the strategies of others. Encourage students to discuss their methods, and emphasize that there are many useful strategies.

Introduce the lesson by facilitating a discussion about the mathematics students have explored during this unit. Ask questions, such as:

Q. **What mathematics have you and your partner explored in the previous lessons?**

Q. **What happens when you add 10 to or subtract 10 from any number? When you add 11 to or subtract 11 from any two-digit number?**

Write the following number sentence where all can see. Ask students to solve it mentally and then talk with their partner about how they did it.

$$7 + 4 + 2 + 6 + 1 + 1 = \underline{\quad}$$

Mathematical Emphasis

Operations can be carried out in a variety of ways.

Have several students share their strategies with the class, and ask:

Q. **Who else did it this way?**

Q. **What is another way someone added these numbers?**

Repeat the activity with the following problems.

$$5 + 6 + 9 + 1 + 4 + 5 = \underline{\quad}$$

$$3 + 2 + 0 + 8 + 9 + 1 = \underline{\quad}$$

For example, in the number sentence
$5 + 6 + 9 + 1 + 4 + 5 = \underline{\quad}$
show:

 $5 + 5 = 10$
 $6 + 4 = 10$
 $9 + 1 = 10$
 so, $10 + 10 + 10 = 30$

Stress that adding compatible numbers is one of many strategies and may not always be the most efficient strategy. Encourage students to decide how to add a set of numbers depending on the numbers and the situation.

If students do not suggest adding the compatible (or "friendly") numbers, demonstrate adding the numbers that total 10 and then adding those 10s.

Do several more examples.

Write the following number sentence and ask pairs to discuss how they might solve it:

$$12$$
$$65$$
$$35$$
$$+\ 88$$

Have pairs share their strategies. Repeat the activity with the following number sentence:

$$90 + 72 + 4 + 10 + 28 = \_\_$$

For example, in the number sentence $90 + 72 + 4 + 28 + 10 = \_\_$ you can add as follows:

$$90 + 10 = 100$$
$$72 + 28 = 100$$
$$\text{so, } 100 + 100 + 4 = 204$$

Note that students may not have enough crayons to mark each pair of numbers with a different color. They will need to use the same color for some pairs.

If students do not suggest adding the friendly numbers, demonstrate, as an additional strategy, adding the numbers that total 100 and then adding the 100s.

Show the Hundred Chart transparency. Explain that pairs will find and mark, using different-colored crayons, all the compatible pairs of numbers that add to 100 on a Hundred Chart. Demonstrate finding and color-coding a few of the compatible number pairs (such as 45 and 55) that add to 100 and writing the number sentences for those compatible numbers (for example, $45 + 55 = 100$).

Facilitate a discussion about how pairs might work. Ask questions, such as:

Q. What are some problems pairs might have? What are fair (or caring or responsible) **ways pairs might deal with these problems?**

Q. Why is it important to explain your thinking and to listen to your partner's thinking?

Social Emphasis

Analyze why it is important to be fair, caring, and responsible.

Observe pairs and, when appropriate, ask questions, such as:

Q. **What other compatible or friendly numbers can you find?**

Q. **How are you making sure you each understand why the numbers you have chosen are compatible?**

Q. **How are you explaining your thinking to your partner?**

●● In pairs, students

1. Find and mark all of the compatible pairs of numbers that add to 100 on a Hundred Chart.

2. Write number sentences with the compatible numbers.

As a class, discuss questions, such as:

Q. **What are some compatible pairs of numbers that add to 100? Did any pair find others?** (List the compatible numbers.)

Q. **What do you notice about the numbers you have marked on the Hundred Chart?**

If number patterns are not mentioned in the discussion, ask:

Some possible patterns that students might notice are:

- In each pair of compatible numbers, the numbers in the ones place add to 10.
- In each pair of compatible numbers, the numbers in the tens place add to 9.
- If you find all the sets of two addends that total 100 on the Hundred Chart, you will have 49 equations. For example, the equations could start with 1 + 99, 2 + 98, 3 + 97, 4 + 96, ... and follow this pattern, ending with the equation 49 + 51.

Q. **Look at the Hundred Chart with the compatible numbers colored in. Do you see any patterns? If so, what patterns do you see?**

Q. **How might finding compatible numbers help you add?**

Help pairs reflect on how they work together. Ask questions, such as:

Q. **If someone were to interview you about how your pair works together, what would you say?**

To help students further develop strategies for adding numbers, have pairs investigate the activities suggested in the Extensions section before going on to the next lesson.

●● ●●

●● ●●

For Pairs That Finish Early

- Have pairs circle and connect sets of two numbers that total 100 on the "Friendly Numbers: Extension" group record sheet. Ask pairs to design similar group record sheets. Have pairs exchange the group record sheets they designed with other pairs and complete them.

For the Next Day

- Have pairs write a different addition problem, with 3 or 4 two-digit addends, on each of 10 index cards. For example:

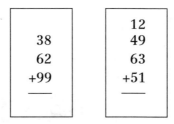

Have pairs exchange their sets of addition problems with another pair. Ask pairs to estimate the answers to the problems and sort the addition problems into the following categories: Less than 100; More than 100 but less than 200; More than 200 but less than 300; and Other. Write several of the students' problems where all can see and, as a class, discuss how and why pairs chose the methods they did for sorting the problems.

Friendly Numbers
Extension

Find, circle, and connect pairs of numbers that total 100.

27

82

85

47

73

63

53

48

18

14

37

52

15

86

     © Developmental Studies Center

Money!

Students add and subtract numbers using coins and look for and discuss patterns. This lesson may take more than one class period.

DAYS AHEAD
3

Mathematical Emphasis

In this lesson, students

- Explore number patterns.
- Add and subtract numbers using coins.

Students add to their understanding that

- Numbers can be composed and decomposed.
- Once a rule to generate a pattern has been identified, the pattern can usually be extended.

Social Emphasis

In this lesson, students

- Use materials responsibly.
- Share the work.
- Explain their thinking.

Students continue to

- Develop group skills.
- Analyze why it is important to be fair, caring, and responsible.

Group Size: 2

Teacher Materials

- Transparencies of coins (see Before the Lesson)
- Transparency of "Money!" group record sheet

Student Materials

Each pair needs

- Baggie of coins (see Before the Lesson)
- "Money!" group record sheet

Extension Materials

- "Money! Extension" transparency (see Before the Lesson)

Each pair needs

- Baggie of coins

- For each pair, prepare a baggie of real, paper, or plastic coins consisting of ten pennies, five nickels, ten dimes, four quarters, and two half-dollars (if available). These coins will also be used in the next lesson, "What's in My Pocket?" (Lesson 7).

- Make a transparency of the coin blackline master and cut along the dotted lines.

- For Extensions, make a transparency of the "Money! Extension" blackline master and cut along the dotted lines.

- Provide time for students to explore the coins. As pairs explore, discuss questions, such as:

  Q. How many ways can you make 5¢? 10¢? 25¢?

  Q. What is the greatest number of dimes you could have if you had $1.32? How do you know?

  Q. What is the greatest number of coins you could have if you had 50¢? What is the fewest number? What other combinations of coins could you have if you had 50¢?

  Q. I have seven coins. Together they equal $1.00. What coins could I have?

Notes

The purpose of this lesson is to provide opportunities for students to compute mentally with numbers such as 25 and 50 and to explore the resulting patterns.

Teacher

Introduce the lesson by playing What Did You See? Turn on the overhead projector and place five transparent nickels on it. Turn off the overhead and ask questions, such as:

Q. What did you see?

Q. About how much money was it?

Q. How did you count it?

Turn on the overhead projector and have the class count the amount with you.

Do this activity several times with different assortments of coins.

Students

•• ••

•• ••

Notes	Teacher	Students

Notes

Pairs may choose to use their coins to help them solve these problems.

Have pairs explain their strategies for solving these problems. For example, if you had two quarters, two dimes, two nickels, and two pennies, students might add
25 + 25 = 50;
50 + 20 = 70;
70 + 10 = 80; and
80 + 2 = 82.
Other students might add
50 + 30 + 2 = 82. Have students try strategies other students suggest.

Teacher

Play How Much Do I Have? Say, "I reached in my pocket and this is what I found:

■ 4 quarters and 1 nickel. How much do I have? How did you count it?"

■ 1 penny, 2 dimes, and a quarter. How much do I have? How did you count it?"

■ 4 nickels, 3 dimes, and 1 penny. How much do I have? How did you count it?"

Show the "Money!" transparency and discuss the directions. Ask students how they might work together to solve the problems on their "Money!" group record sheets. If the following ideas are not part of the discussion, you might wish to ask:

Q. How might you use the materials in a responsible and fair way? Why is that important?

Q. How might you share the work?

Q. Why is it important to explain your thinking?

Observe pairs working and, when appropriate, ask questions, such as:

Q. If you add this row of coins, what would be the total? (Point to a row of coins on the group record sheet.)

Q. What patterns do you see? How could they be extended? What other patterns do you notice?

Students

•• ••

•• ••

••

In pairs, students discuss and solve the problems on the "Money!" group record sheet.

•• ••

•• ••

Mathematical Emphasis

Once a rule to generate a pattern has been identified, the pattern can usually be extended.

As students explain their thinking, write their strategies where all can see. For example, for 25 + 25 + 25, students might suggest
20 + 20 + 20 = 60,
5 + 5 + 5 = 15,
60 + 15 = 75, or
3 × 25 = 75.

State a new set of numbers such as 35 + 35 + 15. Ask students to add the numbers using a strategy they heard from someone else. As a class, discuss the strategies students tried and how they worked with that set of numbers.

Social Emphasis

Develop group skills.

Help students reflect on the lesson. First in pairs, and then as a class, discuss questions, such as:

Q. **What pattern(s) do you see? Did anyone find different patterns?**

Q. **What is 25 + 25 + 25? How do you know? Did anyone use a different strategy? Explain.**

Q. **What is 75 + 25 + 25? How do you know? Who used another strategy? Explain.**

Q. **What is 50 + 25 + 50? How do you know? Did anyone use a different strategy? Explain.**

Q. **What is 5 + 25 + 25 + 25? How do you know? Did anyone use a different strategy? Explain.**

Q. **If I have quarters, dimes, and nickels for a total of $1.00, what combination of coins might I have?**

Q. **How is this lesson like others we have done?**

Discuss how pairs worked. Ask questions, such as:

Q. **What did you like about how you worked together? Why?**

Q. **What problems did you have? How could you improve the way you worked together?**

Q. **What can you say about how you handled the coins? Why do you think that?**

For Pairs That Finish Early

■ Have pairs decide on an amount of money, choose a set of coins that equals that amount, and line up the coins. Have students compute the value of the coins forward and backward. For example, if the total is 77¢, the coins could be as follows:

For the Next Day

■ Show the "Money! Extension" transparencies and discuss. For example, show the picture of the kite and ask questions, such as:

Q. How much would two kites cost? Explain your strategy.

Q. If I buy a kite for 35¢ and give the clerk 50¢, what is my change? Explain.

Q. I have $1.50. How many kites can I buy? Explain.

Show the pictures of the kite and the yo-yo, and ask questions, such as:

Q. I have $1.75. Can I buy the kite and the yo-yo? Explain.

Show the picture of the comic book, and ask questions, such as:

Q. If I have $5.00, can I buy two comic books? Three comic books? Explain.

Q. If two comic books cost $3.20, am I paying more or less than $1.15 for each comic book? Explain.

Show the picture of the compact disc, and ask questions, such as:

Q. If I buy two CDs, will I spend more or less than $20.00? Explain.

Q. I have $6.50. How much more money do I need to buy the CD?

Money!

Find the value for each row of coins. Extend the patterns by adding more rows of coins. Talk about the patterns you see.

Coins	Total value
(1¢) (1¢) (1¢) (5¢)	8¢
(1¢) (1¢) (1¢) (5¢) (5¢)	

Coins	Total value
(25¢)	25¢
(25¢) (25¢)	

Coins	Total value
(50¢)	50¢
(50¢) (50¢)	

Make up a problem of your own.

Coins	Total value

Money!
Extension

Kite

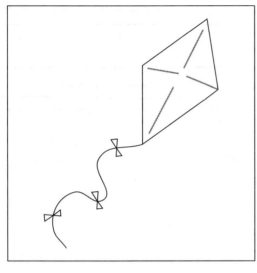

35¢

Yo-yo

53¢

Comic book

$1.60

Compact disc

$12.50

1¢	1¢	1¢	1¢	1¢	1¢
1¢	1¢	1¢	1¢	1¢	1¢
5¢	5¢	5¢	5¢	5¢	5¢
5¢	5¢	5¢	5¢	5¢	5¢
10¢	10¢	10¢	10¢	10¢	10¢
10¢	10¢	10¢	10¢	10¢	10¢
25¢	25¢	25¢	25¢	25¢	25¢
25¢	25¢	25¢	25¢	25¢	25¢
50¢	50¢	50¢	50¢	50¢	50¢
50¢	50¢	50¢	50¢	50¢	50¢

What's in My Pocket?

Students use coins to write and solve riddles about the value of sets of coins. This lesson may take more than one class period.

Mathematical Emphasis

In this lesson, students

- Write and solve riddles.
- Use coins to add and subtract numbers.

Students add to their understanding that

- Numbers can be composed and decomposed.
- Problems may have more than one solution and may be solved in a variety of ways.

Social Emphasis

In this lesson, students

- Share the work.
- Agree on clues for a riddle.
- Explain their thinking.

Students continue to

- Develop group skills.
- Analyze the effect of behavior on others and on the group work.

Group Size: 2

Teacher Materials

- Sentence strips (see Before the Lesson)
- 3 dimes, 2 nickels, and 1 quarter
- Transparencies of coins (from Lesson 6)
- Transparency of "What's in My Pocket?" group record sheet

Student Materials

Each pair needs

- Baggie of coins (from Lesson 6)
- "What's in My Pocket?" group record sheet
- Paper and a pencil

Extension Materials

Each pair needs

- Paper and a pencil

■ Write each line of the following riddles on a sentence strip.

Riddle 1	**Riddle 2**
I have 65¢ in my pocket.	I have 54¢ in my pocket.
I have at least one dime.	I have at least four pennies.
I have one quarter.	I have at least one quarter.
I have six coins in my pocket.	I have eight coins in my pocket.
What coins do I have?	What coins do I have?

■ Have three dimes, two nickels, and a quarter in your pocket for the lesson introduction.

Notes

Students may use coins, illustrations, mental computation, or other strategies to help them solve these riddles.

Provide time for pairs to think about each clue and possible solutions before showing the next clue.

Encourage students to focus on the information provided in each clue and the possible combinations that fit the clues, rather than guessing the exact amount.

The solutions to the riddles on the group record sheet are:

1. One penny, one nickel, three dimes
2. Four pennies, three dimes
3. Four pennies, one dime, three quarters
4. Most: 55¢ – five dimes, one nickel
   Least: 50¢ – four dimes, two nickels

Teacher

Jingle the coins (three dimes, two nickels, and a quarter) in your pocket. State that you have 65¢. Challenge the class to figure out what coins you have. First in pairs, then as a class, have students brainstorm possibilities.

Explain that you have some clues that may help. One at a time, show the sentence strips with the clues for Riddle 1. First in pairs, and then as a class, discuss each clue. Use the transparency coins (from Lesson 6) to illustrate students' responses to questions, such as:

Q. What information does the clue tell us? What coins could I have? How do you know? What are other possibilities?

One at a time, show the clues for Riddle 2. Have pairs discuss each clue before you show the next one. (Note the solution for Riddle 2 is: four pennies, one nickel, two dimes, and one quarter.)

Show the "What's in My Pocket?" transparency and explain the directions. Suggest that pairs might use their coins to help them solve the problems on the "What's in My Pocket" group record sheet. Facilitate a discussion about what might help pairs work together.

Students

●● ●●

●● ●●

Notes	Teacher	Students

Observe pairs working and ask questions, such as:

Q. **What's helping you solve these riddles?**

Q. **How do you know your solution works?**

Q. **How are you explaining your thinking?**

••

In pairs, students discuss and solve the problems on the "What's in My Pocket?" group record sheet.

Have pairs share their solutions. Discuss questions, such as:

Q. **How do you know this solution works?**

Q. **What other solutions also work?**

Explain that pairs will create riddles for other pairs to solve. Direct students' attention to the sentence strips with the two riddles used to introduce the lesson. Analyze the riddles as a class. Discuss how the first clue states the total value of the coins (note that some of the riddles on the "What's in My Pocket?" group record sheet begin with a statement about the number of coins), that each clue reveals one additional bit of information, and that the riddle can be solved with the clues that are given.

Model writing a riddle. Write the following where all can see:

   I have 76¢ in my pocket.

First in pairs, and then as a class, discuss the clue and what collections of coins might be the solution. Pick a solution (such as three quarters and one penny.) Ask:

Q. **What might be a good next clue?**

Continue to develop the riddle, then ask:

•• ••

•• ••

Pairs will need to decide on an amount and a combination of coins that total that amount, then develop their clues.

Q. **What will be important to think about when writing your riddles?**

Notes	Teacher	Students

Observe students and ask yourself questions, such as:

Q. Do students understand that there are many ways to decompose a number? For example,
76 = 25 + 25 + 25 + 1, or
76 = 50 + 25 + 1, or
76 = 10 + 10 + 5 + 50 + 1.

Q. Do students exhibit persistence when exploring clues and possible solutions?

Observe pairs working and, when appropriate, ask questions, such as:

Q. How are you agreeing on how to write your riddle?

Q. How are you making sure the riddle makes sense?

Q. Are there other possible solutions to your riddle? How do you know?

●●

In pairs, students write riddles.

Have pairs exchange riddles with another pair. Have pairs discuss whether the clues make sense. Then ask pairs to solve the riddles and discuss their solutions with the authors of the riddles.

Have several pairs share riddles with the class. First in pairs, then as a class, discuss solutions.

Help students reflect on the lesson by discussing questions, such as:

Q. What was difficult about writing riddles together? Why? What was easy? Why?

Q. How did your behavior affect your partner and the work you did?

Q. What would you do differently next time?

●● ●●

●● ●●

Social Emphasis
Analyze the effect of behavior on others and on the group work.

Extensions

For Pairs That Finish Early

■ Have pairs write a riddle that has more than one answer. Have pairs exchange riddles, find and record all the possible solutions for one another's riddles, and discuss their solutions with the other pair.

For the Next Day

■ Have pairs copy the riddles they wrote and put them into a class book of coin riddles. (Make sure all students have time to contribute at least one riddle to the book.)

What's in My Pocket?

1. I have 36¢ in my pocket.

   I have at least one penny.

   I have five coins in my pocket.

   What are they?

2. I have 34¢ in my pocket.

   I have at least one dime.

   I have no nickels.

   I have seven coins.

   What are they?

3. I have 89¢ in my pocket.

   I have at least four pennies.

   I have eight coins in my pocket.

   What are they?

4. I have 6 coins.

   I have only dimes and nickels.

   I have more dimes than nickels.

   What is the greatest amount of money I could have,

   and what are the coins?

   What is the least amount of money I could have,

   and what are the coins?

Roll the Difference

Students play a game in which they subtract numbers from multiples of one hundred. This lesson may take more than one class period.

DAYS AHEAD
2

Mathematical Emphasis

In this lesson, students will

- Compute using a calculator.
- Use mental computation.
- Look for patterns.

Students add to their understanding that

- Once a rule to generate a pattern has been identified, the pattern can usually be extended.
- Numbers can be composed and decomposed.

Social Emphasis

In this lesson, students

- Explain their thinking.
- Use materials responsibly.

Students continue to

- Develop group skills.

Group Size: 2

Teacher Materials

- Overhead spinner (see Before the Lesson)
- Transparencies of "Roll the Difference" and "Number Sentences" group record sheets

Student Materials

Each pair needs

- Die and spinner (see Before the Lesson)
- "Roll the Difference" group record sheet
- Calculator
- "Number Sentences" group record sheet

Extension Materials

Each pair needs

- Die and spinner (see Before the Lesson)
- "Roll the Difference" group record sheet
- Calculator

- For each pair, make a die numbered as follows: 1, 5, 10, 50, 99, 101. For Extensions, label a die for each pair as follows: 2, 10, 25, 75, 98, 102. (Write the numbers on adhesive dots and place the dots on dice or color cubes.)

- Make a spinner for each pair by copying the spinner face blackline master (see "Directions for Making Spinners," p. 30, for instructions).

- Make a spinner for the overhead by copying the spinner face blackline master on a transparency. Label the overhead spinner like the students' spinners.

Notes	Teacher	Students

Teacher

Introduce the lesson by asking students if they have ever played a game with dice. Ask questions, such as:

Q. When have you ever played a dice game? What did you like about the game?

Explain that today pairs will play a game called Roll the Difference.

Show the "Roll the Difference" transparency and ask a student to play the following game with you as you model it on the overhead projector.

1. One partner spins the spinner and writes the number on the "Roll the Difference" group record sheet in the "Multiple of 100" column.

2. The other partner rolls the die and writes the number in the "Number Rolled" column.

3. Together, partners predict the difference between the number rolled on the die and the multiple of 100 and write the prediction in the "Predicted Difference" column.

4. Together, partners use a calculator to find the actual difference and write it in the "Actual Difference" column.

Notes

For example, Teddy spins 400 on the spinner and writes 400 on the group record sheet. Eiko rolls 101 on the die and writes 101 on the group record sheet. Teddy and Eiko predict that 399 is the answer to 400 – 101 and write their prediction on the group record sheet. They check their prediction with their calculator and record the actual difference of 299 on their group record sheet.

Notes	Teacher	Students

Social Emphasis
Develop appropri-
ate group skills.

Ask students to discuss what they noticed about how you and your partner worked together. Ask questions, such as:

Q. **What helped us work well?**

Q. **What might you suggest to help us work even better?**

Q. **How did we use the materials in a responsible way?**

•• ••

•• ••

Observe pairs playing the game and, when appropriate, ask questions, such as:

Q. **Why do you think this prediction makes sense?**

Q. **How are you both participating?**

••

In pairs, students play Roll the Difference.

Have several pairs report some of the results from their game. Write these where all can see. Ask questions, such as:

Q. **Were your predictions reasonable? How do you know? Did they become more reasonable? Why?**

Q. **What patterns do you see?**

Show the "Number Sentences" trans-parency. Ask pairs to discuss and record solutions to the problems on their "Number Sentences" group record sheet.

•• ••

•• ••

| **Notes** | **Teacher** | **Students** |

Observe students and informally assess how they solve the equations. Ask yourself questions, such as:

Q. Can students compute by decomposing numbers?
Q. Do students rely on standard algorithms for subtraction?
Q. Do students use different mental computation strategies? If so, what are they?
Q. Can students verbalize why they use different strategies for different problems?

Observe pairs and, when appropriate, ask questions, such as:

Q. What strategies are you using to solve these problems?

Q. When you subtracted 101 from 600, the answer was 499. If you subtracted 301 from 600, what would the answer be? How do you know?

Q. What patterns do you notice?

Q. How are you making sure your partner understands your ideas?

••

In pairs, students discuss and record solutions to the problems on the "Number Sentences" group record sheet.

A cooperative structure such as "Think, Pair, Share" (see p. xii) can provide opportunities for all students to be involved in the discussion.

Have pairs report their solutions as you write them on the "Number Sentences" transparency. First in pairs, then as a class, have students discuss the patterns they see. Encourage students to explain and justify their thinking.

Help students reflect on the lesson. Ask questions, such as:

Q. How does playing this game help you with subtraction?

Q. If you were to tell someone about why your partner is a terrific partner, what are some things you would say?

•• ••

•• ••

 **Extensions**

For Pairs That Finish Early

■ Have pairs play Roll the Difference again. Note if students' predictions become progressively more accurate.

For the Next Day

■ Have pairs play Roll the Difference using a die with different numbers, such as 2, 20, 25, 75, 98, 102.

Names

Roll the Difference

Multiple of 100	Number Rolled	Predicted Difference	Actual Difference

Number Sentences

300 – 101 = ____	700 – 5 = ____	400 – 10 = ____
500 – 101 = ____	200 – 5 = ____	100 – 10 = ____
700 – 101 = ____	500 – 5 = ____	800 – 10 = ____
200 – 101 = ____	900 – 5 = ____	600 – 10 = ____
500 – 50 = ____	200 – 99 = ____	900 – 1 = ____
300 – 50 = ____	300 – 99 = ____	600 – 1 = ____
800 – 50 = ____	900 – 99 = ____	200 – 1 = ____
400 – 50 = ____	100 – 99 = ____	500 – 1 = ____

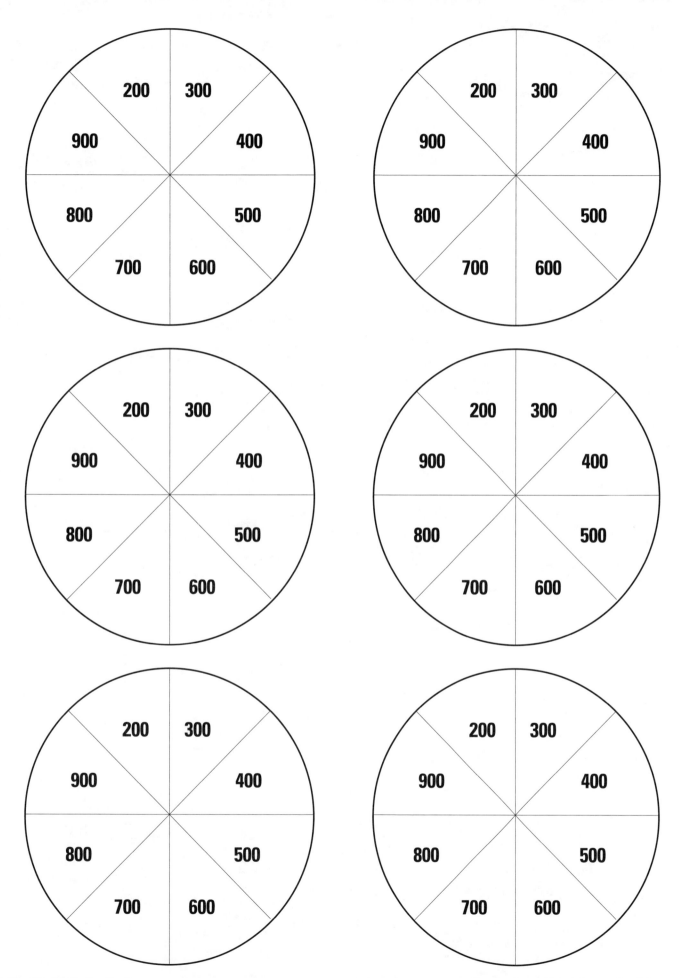

Shake, Rattle, and Toss

Students predict the outcome of tossing a penny one hundred times, then toss the penny and record their results. Students analyze the class data and compute the number of heads and the number of tails.

DAYS AHEAD
1

Teacher Materials

- Class chart (see Before the Lesson)
- Penny
- Paper cup
- Transparency of the "Shake, Rattle, and Toss" direction sheet

Mathematical Emphasis

In this lesson, students

- Collect, organize, and analyze data.
- Compute informally.

Students add to their understanding that

- Questions about our world can be asked, and data about those questions can be collected, organized, and analyzed.
- Making a reasonable estimate requires gathering and using information.
- Numbers can be composed and decomposed.
- Operations can be carried out in a variety of ways.

Social Emphasis

In this lesson, students

- Share the work.
- Record accurately.
- Make decisions.
- Include everyone.

Students continue to

- Develop group skills.

Group Size: 4

Student Material

Each group of four needs

- Penny
- "Shake, Rattle, and Toss" direction sheet
- Paper cup
- Paper and a pencil
- Access to a calculator

Extension Material

Each group of four needs

- Paper and a pencil
- Lima bean painted on one side, or any other two-sided counter

■ Make the following chart for recording the results of the groups' penny tosses:

Heads	Tails

Notes	Teacher	Students

Introduce the lesson by combining pairs to form groups of four. Ask groups to look at and make observations about their penny. Discuss these observations and ask questions, such as:

Q. When you toss a penny, what could the result be?

Q. If you toss a penny 100 times, will one side come up more frequently than the other, or will both sides come up the same number of times? (Have pairs record their predictions.)

Explain that groups will toss a penny 100 times, record the outcome for each toss, and then compute the number of heads and the number of tails.

Demonstrate shaking the coin in a paper cup, gently tossing the coin on the desk, and recording a tally mark for heads or tails.

Show the "Shake, Rattle, and Toss" direction sheet transparency, and discuss the following directions.

1. Toss the coin 20 times. Record a tally mark for each toss.

2. Review your original prediction for 100 tosses and make a new prediction if you wish.

3. Continue to toss the penny until you have tossed it a total of 100 times.

4. Compute the number of heads and tails for the 100 tosses.

Notes	**Teacher**	**Students**

	Facilitate a discussion about cooperative ways to work. Ask questions, such as:	
Social Emphasis Develop group skills.	**Q. How might you share the work?**	
	Q. How can you be sure everyone is included?	
	Q. How can you be sure you are recording your results accurately?	

	Observe groups and, when appropriate, ask questions, such as:	In groups, students
Observe students and ask yourself questions, such as:	**Q. What is the result of the first 20 tosses of your penny?**	1. Toss a penny 20 times and record the outcome for each toss.
Q. Do students use the information gained from the first 20 tosses to predict the outcome of the 100 tosses? If so, how? (Note: some students may not use a referent when making their prediction. Do not force the issue.)	**Q. What did you predict for the 100 tosses? Was your prediction reasonable? Why?**	2. Review their original prediction for tossing a penny 100 times, revise if desired, and record.
		3. Continue until they have tossed the penny a total of 100 times.
Q. Do students have a sense of how reasonable their prediction is?		4. Compute the total number of heads and tails for the 100 tosses.

	Ask groups to report their number of heads and tails. Record these totals on the class chart.	
	First in groups, and then as a class, discuss questions, such as:	
Students might notice that the difference between the results is small, that the data cluster around one number, or that several groups had similar results.	**Q. Look at the results on the class chart. What do you notice about the number of heads and the number of tails?**	
	Q. Are any of the results unusual? Which ones? Why do you think that happened?	

Notes

Encourage groups to compute mentally or to use informal strategies for finding the total number of heads and tails. For example, some groups might add a column of numbers by first adding all the compatible numbers, and some groups might add pairs of numbers and combine the sums (with or without a calculator) to find the total. Other groups might add the numbers in the 10s column first and then add the 1s. Write the groups' strategies where all can see and discuss them. Have students try each other's strategies.

Teacher

Q. **How many of the total number of tosses were tails?**

Q. **What strategy did your group use to compute the number of tails? Did any group use a different strategy?**

Q. **How many of the total number of tosses were heads?**

Q. **What strategy did your group use to compute the number of heads? Did any group use a different strategy?**

Help students reflect on the group work. Ask questions, such as:

Q. **What decisions did your group make before you began to toss the penny? How did that affect your work?**

Q. **What did you like about the way your group worked?**

Students

For Groups That Finish Early

For the Next Day

Extensions

■ Have students discuss and solve the following problem:

   If each student in the class tossed a coin 100 times, how many tosses would the class make?

■ Give each group a lima bean painted on one side (or any other two-sided counter) and ask: "If you toss the lima bean 100 times, will one side come up more frequently than the other? Will both sides come up the same number of times? What do you think will happen? Why?"

Have groups

1. Predict the outcome of tossing the lima bean 100 times and record the prediction.

2. Toss the lima bean 100 times and record the outcome for each toss.

3. Compute the total number of times each side comes up.

4. Compare the prediction for the 100 tosses with the actual outcome.

5. Discuss how this activity is similar to or different from the penny toss activity in Lesson 8.

Shake, Rattle, and Toss
Direction Sheet

1. Toss the coin 20 times. Record a tally mark for
each toss.

2. Review your original prediction for 100 tosses and
make a new prediction if you wish.

3. Continue to toss the penny until you have tossed it
a total of 100 times.

4. Compute the number of heads and tails for the
100 tosses.

Mental Math!

Students write and solve problems that can be solved by using mental computation and then reflect on their work together in this unit.

Transition Emphasis

In this lesson, students

- Write and solve problems.
- Use mental computation to solve problems.
- Reflect on how they worked together.

Students add to their understanding that

- Numbers can be composed and decomposed.

Social Emphasis

In this lesson, students

- Express their feelings about working together.
- Agree on a problem to write.

Students continue to

- Develop group skills.
- Analyze the effect of behavior on others and on the group work.

Group Size: 2

Student Materials

Each pair needs

- Paper and a pencil

Extension Materials

- At least 2 index cards for each pair and a box to hold them

Introduce the lesson by facilitating a class discussion about the unit. Discuss questions, such as:

Q. What did you think about this unit?

Q. What did you learn about working cooperatively with your partner?

Q. What mathematics did you explore during this unit?

Q. What was your favorite activity? Why? What was your least favorite activity? Why?

For example, students might say: numbers that total ten, numbers ending in five, multiples of ten and 100, doubles, 25, 50, etc.

Introduce the lesson by asking students what numbers they think might be easy to add and subtract mentally. As students mention numbers, check for agreement or disagreement on the part of the class, and list the numbers that the class thinks are easy to add and subtract.

Explain that pairs will write problems, using the numbers suggested by students, that others should be able to solve in their heads without using paper and pencil or a calculator. Explain that the problems will be collected and put into a "Class Problem Kit."

Ask students to choose some numbers. Model writing several problems, such as:

> Jaime had 25¢. He wants to buy a comic book for $1.50. How much more money does he need?

> Fatima had 30 paperback books in her library. She gave 15 of them to her classroom's library. Then she bought 5 new books. How many books does she have now?

Facilitate a discussion about the problems. Ask questions, such as:

Q. Was it easy to do these problems without paper and pencil or a calculator? Why?

Q. Do the problems make sense? Why?

Notes	Teacher	Students
	Q. How do the problems end?	•• ••
	Q. What will be important to think about when writing your problems?	•• ••

	Observe pairs working and, when appropriate, ask questions, such as:	••
		In pairs, students write problems that can be solved mentally.
	Q. How are you agreeing on what to write?	
	Q. How are you making sure the problem makes sense?	
	Q. What strategies could be used to solve this problem?	

Discuss ways to be caring and respectful when commenting on others' work and why this is important.	**H**ave several pairs share their problems with the class. First in pairs, then as a class, discuss the problems and possible solutions. Ask questions, such as:	•• •• •• ••
	Q. Is this problem easy to add [subtract] mentally? Why?	
	Q. Does this problem make sense? If not, how could it be made clearer?	
	Q. How did you solve this problem? Did anyone do it another way? How?	
Social Emphasis Analyze the effect of behavior on others and on the group work.	Help students reflect on the lesson and how they worked together during the unit by asking questions, such as:	
	Q. What was difficult about working together? What was easy? Why?	
	Q. How did your behavior affect your partner and the work you did?	
	Q. What did you learn about working together that might help other pairs work together?	
	Give students an opportunity to thank each other and to share with each other what they liked about working together.	

Extensions

For Pairs That Finish Early

- Have pairs choose two of the problems they wrote, copy them on index cards (with the answer on the back of the card), and put it into a box labeled "Class Problem Kit."

For the Next Day

- If all pairs have not contributed problems to the "Class Problem Kit" suggested above, provide time for them to do so.

- Give students time to solve and discuss the problems in the kit. (You might also use the problems in the kit as five-minute mental math problems at the beginning or end of future math periods.)

Data Analysis and Number Sense

Mathematical Development

This unit provides students with opportunities to explore number in the context of analyzing data about pets. Students collect, organize, and interpret data; group and count data; make estimates; compute mentally; write and solve problems about pets; and decide which method of calculation (mental computation, calculator, paper and pencil, or a combination of methods) is the most appropriate for adding particular sets of data. The unit also makes use of literature and resource materials to enrich students' experiences. Students have opportunities to read and write stories, to research information, and to draw pictures about pets.

Social Development

The social focus of this unit is to provide opportunities for students to analyze how their behavior and the behavior of others affects their group work and interaction. Students discuss ways to work with a partner and are encouraged to solve problems, to reach agreements that both students find acceptable, to explain their thinking, to check their own and their partner's understanding, and to help each other. Open-ended questions also encourage students to examine how they work in responsible ways.

Students should be randomly assigned to pairs that work together throughout the unit.

Mathematical Emphasis

Conceptually, experiences in this unit help students construct their understanding that

- Questions about our world can be asked, and data about those questions can be collected, organized, and analyzed.

- Problems may have more than one solution and may be solved in a variety of ways.

- Choosing a process for making calculations depends on the numbers themselves and how the results will be used.

- Operations can be carried out in a variety of ways.

- Numbers can be used to describe quantities.

- Making a reasonable estimate requires gathering and using information.

- Measurement is approximate. Objects can be measured by making direct comparisons.

- Logical reasoning can be used to solve problems.

Social Emphasis

Socially, experiences in this unit help students to

- Develop group skills.

- Analyze the effect of behavior on others and on the group work.

- Relate the values of fairness, caring, and responsibility to behavior.

- Take responsibility for learning and behavior.

Lessons

This unit includes eight lessons. The calendar icon indicates that some preparation is needed or that an experience is suggested for students prior to that lesson.

1. Our Unusual Pets
(page 145)

Introductory team-building lesson in which pairs draw a picture of and write about an unusual pet they would like to have.

2. Do You Have a Pet?
(page 151)

Graphing lesson in which pairs analyze data about whether students own a pet and about the number of pets students have, and then write statements summarizing the data.

3. How Many Pets?
(page 157)

Informal computation lesson in which pairs choose an appropriate method for calculating the number of pets students in the class own.

4. Pets, Pets, Pets!
(page 161)

Graphing lesson in which pairs collect and analyze data about the number of each kind of pet students own and write statements summarizing the data.

5. Pet Problems
(page 167)

Problem-solving lesson in which pairs write and solve problems using information from the graphs developed in previous lessons.

6. Facts About Pets
(page 171)

Problem-solving lesson in which pairs measure themselves and compute informally to solve problems comparing their height to the height of a pony.

7. Pet Show
(page 177)

Problem-solving lesson in which pairs compute informally and use logical reasoning to solve problems about a pet show.

8. Fantasy Pets
(page 187)

Transition lesson in which pairs create a fantasy pet and reflect on their work together.

Materials

The materials needed for the unit are listed below. The first page of each lesson lists the materials specific to that lesson. All blackline masters for transparencies and group record sheets are included at the end of each lesson. Transparencies and other materials are available in the *Number Power* Package for Grade 3.

Throughout the unit, you will need access to an overhead projector, and students will need access to supplies such as calculators, scissors, crayons, rulers, glue sticks, paper, and pencil. While it is important that calculators be available at all times, they are listed on the first page of the lessons for which they are particularly important. If possible, each group should have a container with these supplies available to use at their discretion.

Teacher Materials

- Books about pets (see p. 144; Lessons 1 and 8)
- Materials for forming pairs (Lesson 1)
- Transparency of "Our Unusual Pets" direction sheet (Lesson 1)
- Graph titled "Do You Have a Pet?" (Lessons 2, 4, and 5)
- Graph titled "How Many Pets Do You Have?" (Lessons 2, 3, 4, and 5)
- Self-adhesive dots (Lessons 2 and 4)
- *A Rose for Pinkerton* by Steven Kellogg (New York: The Dial Press, 1981) (Lesson 2)
- Graph titled "How Many of Each of These Pets Do You Have?" (Lessons 4 and 5)
- Transparency of "Facts About Pets" group record sheet (Lesson 6)
- Transparency of "A Pet Show Graph" (Lesson 7)
- Transparency of "Pet Show" group record sheet (Lesson 7)
- *The Whingdingdilly* by Bill Peet (Boston: Houghton Mifflin Company, Inc., 1970) (Lesson 8)
- Drawing paper (Lesson 8)

Student Materials

Each student needs

- 8½″ × 11″ drawing paper (Lesson 1)

Each pair needs

- Calculator (Lessons 3, 5, 6, and 7)
- "Pet Show" group record sheet (Lesson 7)

Student Materials *(continued)*

- "Facts About Pets" group record sheet (Lesson 6)
- Yardstick or inch tape measure (Lesson 6)
- "A Pet Show Graph" (Lesson 7)
- Drawing paper (Lesson 8)

Extension Materials

- *Can I Keep Him?* by Steven Kellogg (New York: Dial Press for Young Readers, 1971) (Lesson 1)
- *I Want a Dog* by Dayal Kaur Khalsa (New York: Crown Publishers, 1987) (Lesson 2)
- Books about pets (see p. 144; Lesson 4)
- Box to hold index cards (Lesson 5)

Each pair needs

- 2 index cards (Lesson 5)
- Calculator (Lesson 5)
- Drawing paper (Lessons 6 and 8)
- "A Pet Show Graph" (Lesson 7)
- "Pet Show: Extension" group record sheet (Lesson 7)

Each student needs

- Drawing paper (Lesson 4)

Teaching Hints

- Prior to each lesson, think about open-ended questions you might ask to extend and probe the thinking of your students. Decide which Extensions to have ready for pairs that finish early.

- During the unit students will organize data on graphs. As graphs are completed, save them or keep them posted in a visible location for use in subsequent lessons.

- Have books, poems, encyclopedias, and magazine articles available for students to read about animals and pets. See the bibliography on page 6 for suggested books about pets. An excellent resource is *The Kids' World Almanac of Animals and Pets* by Deborah G. Felder (New York: World Almanac, 1989).

- Throughout the unit, there are numerous opportunities for students to research information about animals and pets. A different focus is suggested in each instance. For example, in Lesson 1, students research information about animals that would make unusual pets; in Lesson 4, pairs research information about pet care; and in Lesson 8, pairs create a fantasy pet by combining three different pets and research facts about their pets. You may want to make a class book with students' work.

- In this unit, students are frequently asked to explain their thinking to their partners and to the class. Many lessons suggest that you encourage students to verbalize their thinking and that you ask follow-up questions to help them more fully articulate their understanding. Recognize, however, that some students will have difficulty doing so. Provide many opportunities for students to not only talk about their thinking and to hear the thinking of others but to model, illustrate, or demonstrate their thinking.

- Consider taking the class to a pet store, or inviting a member of the local Humane Society to visit the class to talk about pets and pet care.

- Have calculators available at all times for students to use when they choose. Periodically ask if any students used calculators for their work and lead an informal discussion about their use and why they chose to use them.

- After each lesson, review any Extensions that students have not explored and decide whether to have students investigate these Extensions before going on to the next lesson.

Assessment Techniques

These informal assessment techniques will help you assess your students' understanding of and ability to make reasonable estimates, to determine one-half of a set of data, and to compute informally. Their purpose is not to determine mastery. Students' understanding will vary from experience to experience, particularly as they begin to construct an understanding of number and operations.

Use the following assessment techniques throughout the unit. As you observe, note students' conceptual understanding as well as their behavior (for example, some students may give up easily or exhibit a lack of confidence). Before the lessons, develop some open-ended questions or decide on an area on which to focus your observations such as those suggested below and in the lessons. Be open to students' responses, and probe their thinking by asking follow-up questions that require them to explain further. Whenever possible, record students' responses. Compare students' responses over time to assess growth in their conceptual understanding.

Observe Individual Students Working

As students work, observe individual students and ask yourself questions, such as:

> **Q. Does the student make reasonable estimates? Can the student use logic to explain the reasonableness of an estimate? Does the student base his or her estimate on available information?**

If a student chooses not to gather and use information to make an estimate, do not force the issue. Some students will need many experiences estimating and discussing the reasons for their estimates before they experience the logic of using information in order to make a reasonable estimate.

> **Q. Can the student mentally compute fractional parts of data such as one-half of a set?** (For example 36 out of 72 people surveyed have a pet. One-half of the people surveyed have a pet.) **Does the student demonstrate an understanding that all the students together represent the whole, and that half of that whole can be computed?**

Students may need many opportunities to explore a whole set of data and fractional parts of the set of data. Provide students with opportunities to explore sets of data, to mentally compute one half of the set of data, and to discuss their strategies with each other.

> **Q. Does the student use a variety of strategies to solve computation problems?**

Observe how flexible a student is with number and operations. Notice whether the student uses the standard algorithm for all situations, or computes informally or mentally when appropriate. Notice when the student chooses to use a calculator and whether the student has a sense of the reasonableness of their calculations when they use the calculator.

Student Writing

Throughout the unit, ask students to verbalize their thinking and at times to explain their thinking in writing. During this unit, students write to

- Describe, analyze, and summarize data.
- Explain the strategies they use to compute and solve problems.
- Create their own pet stories.
- List facts about pets.
- Create word problems.

Bibliography

Stories About Pets

Brett, Jan. *The First Dog*. New York: Trumpet, 1988.

Kellogg, Steven. *A Rose for Pinkerton*. New York: Dial Press, 1981.

——— . *Can I Keep Him?* New York: Dial Books for Young Readers, 1971.

——— . *Pinkerton, Behave!* New York: Dial Books for Young Readers, 1971.

——— . *Prehistoric Pinkerton*. New York: Dial Books for Young Readers, 1987.

Khalsa, Dayal Kaur. *I Want a Dog*. New York: Crown Publishers, Inc., 1987.

Naylor, Phyllis R. *Shiloh*. New York: Dell Publishing, 1991.

Peet, Bill. *The Whingdingdilly*. Boston: Houghton Mifflin Company, 1970.

Smyth, Gwenda. *A Pet for Mrs. Arbuckle*. New York: Crown Publishers, Inc. 1981.

Viorst, Judith. *The Tenth Good Thing About Barney*. New York: Aladdin, 1971.

Yamashima, Mitsu, and Taro Yamashima. *Momo's Kitten*. New York: Puffin Books, 1977.

Resource Books About Pets

Evans, Mark. *The American Society for the Prevention of Cruelty to Animals' Pet Care Guides for Kids—Guinea Pig*. New York: Dorling Kindersley, Inc., 1992.

——— . *The American Society for the Prevention of Cruelty to Animals' Pet Care Guides for Kids—Kitten*. New York: Dorling Kindersley, Inc., 1992.

——— . *The American Society for the Prevention of Cruelty to Animals' Pet Care Guides for Kids—Puppy*. New York: Dorling Kindersley, Inc., 1992.

——— . *The American Society for the Prevention of Cruelty to Animals' Pet Care Guides for Kids—Rabbit*. New York: Dorling Kindersley, Inc., 1992.

Felder, Deborah G. *The Kids' World Almanac of Animals and Pets*. New York: World Almanac, 1989.

Fritzche, Helga. *Cats*. New York: Barron's Educational Series, Inc., 1982.

Hawsley, Gerald and Julie Hawsley. *Small Pets*. New York: Mallard Press, 1989.

McHattie, Grace. *Kitten Care for Children*. London, England: Andre Deutsch Limited, 1989.

Palmer, Joan. *Know Your Pets, Aquarium Fish*. New York, NY: The Boatwright Press, 1989.

——— . *Know Your Pets, Cats*. New York: The Boatwright Press, 1989.

——— . *Know Your Pets, Dogs*. New York: The Boatwright Press, 1989.

——— . *Know Your Pets, Hamsters*. New York: The Boatwright Press, 1989.

——— . *Know Your Pets, Rabbits*. New York: The Boatwright Press, 1989.

Ricciuti, Edward R. *Shelf Pets*. New York: Harper and Row Publishers, 1971.

Stevens, Carla. *Your First Pet and How to Take Care of It*. New York: Macmillan Publishing Company, Inc., 1974.

Weber, William J. *Care of Uncommon Pets*. New York: DMV Holt, Rinehart and Winston, 1979.

Our Unusual Pets

Students draw a picture of and write about an unusual pet they would like to have. Students then introduce their partner to the class and share information about their partner's unusual pet. This lesson may take more than one class period.

Team Builder Emphasis

In this lesson, students

- Meet and work with their partner.
- Begin to develop an effective working relationship.

Students add to their understanding that

- Numbers can be used to describe quantities.

Social Emphasis

In this lesson, students

- Listen to each other.
- Ask for help when needed.
- Give help when asked.

Students continue to

- Develop group skills.

Group Size: 2

Teacher Materials

- Books about pets (see Before the Lesson)
- Materials for forming pairs (see Before the Lesson)
- Transparency of "Our Unusual Pets" direction sheet

Student Materials

Each student needs

- 8½″ × 11″ sheet of drawing paper
- Crayons or markers
- Paper and a pencil

Extension Materials

- *Can I Keep Him?* (see Extensions)

Each pair needs

- Paper and a pencil

My partner's name is Solomon. He'd like to have a Hippopotamus as a pet.

- Collect resource books about animals and pets. (See the bibliography on p. 144 for suggestions.)

- Two days prior to this lesson, explain that the class will spend the next several weeks investigating facts about pets. Lead a brief discussion about common pets. Then ask:

  Q. If you could pick an unusual pet, what might you pick? Why?

  Explain that students will have time to do some research in order to find out more about animals, to pick an unusual pet, and to gather facts about this pet.

  Provide sufficient time for students to read about and discuss animals, to choose an unusual pet, and to gather and record facts about it.

- Decide how you will form pairs to work together during the unit. (See Forming Groups, page xiii, for random-grouping suggestions.) Prepare any materials needed.

Notes

This lesson serves several purposes. First, it is designed to be a team builder that provides an opportunity for students to get to know their partner and to develop a working relationship. Second, it is designed to capture students' imaginations and to involve them in the theme of the unit.

Teacher

Form pairs using the activity you have chosen. Explain that pairs will work together during this unit as the class explores data about pets.

Introduce the lesson by telling a story, such as:

> The other day I read a newspaper article about a woman who owns a pig as a pet. The woman said her pig weighed about 150 pounds and was 2 years old. She said that pigs are very intelligent, like to eat leftovers, and make great pets. She and her pig like to go for walks and when it is hot out she likes to watch her pig roll around in the mud.

Ask:

Q. You have had several days to read about different animals. What animal did you choose to be your unusual pet? Why?

Students

●● ●●

●● ●●

Notes	**Teacher**	**Students**

Have books about animals available to students.

Show the "Our Unusual Pets" direction sheet transparency. Explain that students will discuss their unusual pet with their partner, then:

1. Draw a picture of their pet.

2. Write some interesting facts about their pet.

3. Write about why they would like to have the animal as a pet.

4. Show what they have written and drawn to their partner, making sure they are ready to tell the class about each other's pet.

Explain that the pet pictures and written information will be put into a class book about unusual pets.

Social Emphasis
Develop group skills.

Suggest that students might need help writing about their unusual pets. Facilitate a discussion about how students might ask their partner for help and how partners might help each other.

●● ●●

●● ●●

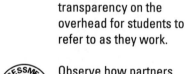

Leave the "Our Unusual Pets" direction sheet transparency on the overhead for students to refer to as they work.

Observe how partners interact. Note positive interactions and any problems you might discuss when the class reflects on the lesson.

Observe pairs working and, when appropriate, ask questions, such as:

Q. Is your partner helping you write? How? How does that make you feel?

Q. How are you making sure you understand what your partner is telling you about his or her unusual pet?

●● In pairs, students

1. Discuss their unusual pets.

2. Individually draw a picture of and write about their pet.

3. Show what they have written and their picture of their unusual pet to their partner and make sure they are ready to tell the class about each other's pet.

Notes	Teacher	Students

Notes

Assure students that during the next several days they will all have an opportunity to share their partner's unusual pet with the class. After all students have shared, put their pictures and information in a book titled *Our Unusual Pets*.

Teacher

Explain that partners will introduce each other to the class, show their partner's picture, and tell the class about their partner's unusual pet. Provide time for partners to discuss what they will say to the class about each other's unusual pet.

Have several pairs share. Encourage students to ask the pair questions about the animals and why they would like to have them as pets.

First in pairs, then as a class, have students reflect on how they worked with their partner by discussing questions, such as:

Q. Was it easy or hard to share your partner's work with the class? Why?

Q. Why do you think I asked you to share your partner's work instead of your own?

If appropriate, share some of your observations of the positive interaction and problems you noted as pairs worked.

Students

•• ••

•• ••

Extensions

For Pairs That Finish Early

■ Suggest that students get to know their partner. Encourage them to discuss such things as their favorite books, things they like to do, places they like to visit, and people they like to visit.

For the Next Day

■ Have more students share information about their partner's unusual pet. Provide time for students to review with their partner what they will say about each other's unusual pet before they share with the class.

■ Read *Can I Keep Him?* by Steven Kellog (New York: Dial Books for Young Readers, 1971) and facilitate a discussion about the story with the class. Have pairs write a similar story about their unusual pet.

Our Unusual Pets
Directions Sheet

1. Discuss your unusual pet with your partner.

2. On a sheet of drawing paper, draw a picture of your unusual pet.

3. Write some interesting facts about the animal you would like to have as an unusual pet.

4. Write about why you would like to have the animal as a pet.

5. Show what you have written and drawn to your partner. Make sure you are both ready to tell the class about each other's pet.

Lesson 2

Do You Have a Pet?

Students graph data about whether they have a pet and the number of pets they have and then write statements analyzing the data. This lesson may take more than one class period.

DAYS AHEAD
2

Mathematical Emphasis

In this lesson, students

- Graph and interpret data.
- Write statements summarizing data.

Students add to their understanding that

- Questions about our world can be asked, and data about those questions can be collected, organized, and analyzed.
- Making a reasonable estimate requires gathering and using information.

Social Emphasis

In this lesson, students

- Explain their thinking.
- Listen to the thinking of others.
- Agree on statements to write.

Students continue to

- Develop group skills.
- Analyze the effect of behavior on others and on the group work.

Group Size: 2

Teacher Materials

- "Do You Have a Pet?" and "How Many Pets Do You Have?" graphs (see Before the Lesson)
- Self-adhesive dots (see Before the Lesson)
- *A Rose for Pinkerton* (see Before the Lesson)

Student Materials

Each pair needs

- Paper and a pencil

Extension Materials

- *I Want a Dog* (see Extensions)

Each pair needs

- Paper and a pencil

- Make the following graphs on large sheets of paper and post.

Do You Have a Pet?	
Yes	No

How Many Pets Do You Have?

0	1	2	3	4	5	6	7	8	9	10	11	12

- Collect data by having individual students use self-adhesive dots to mark each graph.

- Obtain a copy of *A Rose for Pinkerton* by Steven Kellog (New York: The Dial Press, 1981) or choose one or two books about pets to read to the class. (See the Overview, p. 144, for a bibliography of suggested books about pets.)

Notes	**Teacher**	**Students**
	Read *A Rose for Pinkerton* to the class. Facilitate a discussion about the story. Ask questions, such as:	•• •• •• ••
	Q. Do you have a pet?	
	Q. Is your pet anything like the pet in the story? Explain.	
	Direct students' attention to the two graphs. First in pairs, and then as a class, discuss the data on the graphs. Ask questions, such as:	
A cooperative structure such as "Turn to Your Partner" (see p. xii) provides opportunities for all students to be involved in the discussion.	**Q. What do the data on the "Do You Have a Pet?" graph tell us about our class?**	

Students might suggest grouping and counting the data by groupings such as twos, fives, or tens. Choose one of the counting strategies and have students demonstrate how to count the data using that strategy.

Q. **How might we group the data on the "Do You Have a Pet?" graph to count them more easily?**

Q. **What do the data on the "How Many Pets Do You Have?" graph tell us about our class?**

Q. **Where are the data clumped on the "How Many Pets Do You Have?" graph? Why?**

Q. **Are there any categories without data? Why?**

Q. **Looking at the data on the "Do You Have a Pet?" graph, what statement can you make about our classmates' pets? What statement can you make about what the graph does not tell us about our classmates' pets?**

Q. **Looking at the data on the "How Many Pets Do You Have?" graph, what statement can you make about our classmates' pets? What statement can you make about what the graph does not tell us about our classmates' pets?**

Students might make statements, such as:

- "Most students in our class own pets."
- "We do not know what kinds of pets students have."
- "Nobody in the class owns more than ten pets."
- "Eight students each own two pets."
- "We do not know how many dogs students have as pets."

As students contribute statements, write several where all can see. Discuss each statement and check for agreement on the part of the class. Ask students to explain why they agree or disagree.

Explain that pairs will write three statements about what the data on the graphs tell them and three statements about what the data on the graphs do not tell them about their classmates' pets. Have pairs discuss how they might work together.

Notes	Teacher	Students

Notes

Use pairs' written statements to help you assess students' ability to interpret the data. Students will demonstrate different levels of sophistication when interpreting data.

Teacher

Observe pairs as they write and, when appropriate, ask questions, such as:

Q. What are you and your partner doing that is helping you work together? Do you need to change anything? What might work better?

Q. How do you know your statements make sense?

Students

••

In pairs, students write statements about the data on the "Do You Have a Pet?" and the "How Many Pets Do You Have?" graphs.

Mathematical Emphasis

Questions about our world can be asked, and data about those questions can be collected, organized, and analyzed.

Provide sufficient time for students to explore these questions.

Ask several pairs to share their statements. Discuss them and check for agreement on the part of the class. Ask students to explain why they agree or disagree.

First in pairs, and then as a class, discuss questions, such as:

Q. Do more or less than half of the students in the class have pets? How do you know? Did any pair use a different strategy to solve this problem? Explain.

Q. What are some situations in which you would need to know the exact number of pets people have? When would an estimate be fine?

Q. If we asked all the adults in the school the same questions about their pets and put that information on graphs, do you think their graphs would look similar to our graphs? Why?

Q. Do you think graphs of third graders who live in [cities/country] would look similar to our graphs? Why?

•• ••
•• ••

Social Emphasis

Analyze the effect of behavior on others and on the group work.

Q. In what ways did you and your partner work well together? How has that made you feel about working with each other?

Q. Before you began to write, you and your partner discussed ways to work together. Did you work the way you planned? What happened?

The "How Many Pets Do You Have?" graph will be used in Lessons 3, 4, and 5. The "Do You Have a Pet?" graph will be used in Lessons 4 and 5.

Save both graphs to use in future lessons.

Extensions

For Pairs That Finish Early

- Have pairs discuss and list things they would like to know about their classmates' pets.

For the Next Day

- Read *I Want a Dog* by Dayal Kaur Khalsa (New York: Crown Publishers, Inc., 1987) and facilitate a discussion about the story with the class. First in pairs, then as a class, discuss questions, such as:

  Q. **What does it mean to take care of and be responsible for a pet?**

  Q. **How are you responsible for your pet?**

  Q. **How are you responsible for yourself? How might you take more responsibility for your own behavior?**

- Continue with the next lesson, "How Many Pets?"

How Many Pets?

Students choose a strategy for calculating the number of pets owned by all students in the class.

Mathematical Emphasis

In this lesson, students

- Use mental computation, a calculator, or paper and pencil to compute.

Students add to their understanding that

- Choosing a process for making calculations depends on the numbers themselves and how the results will be used.
- Problems may have more than one solution and may be solved in a variety of ways.

Social Emphasis

In this lesson, students

- Explain their thinking.
- Check for understanding.

Students continue to

- Develop group skills.
- Analyze the effect of behavior on others and on the group work.

Group Size: 2

Teacher Materials

- "How Many Pets Do You Have?" graph (from Lesson 2)

Student Materials

Each pair needs

- Access to a calculator
- Paper and a pencil

Extension Materials

Each pair needs

- Paper and a pencil

Post the "How Many Pets Do You Have?" graph where all can see. Have any students who were absent during Lesson 2 mark the graph.

Provide sufficient time for pairs to explore this question.

First in pairs, and then as a class, review the previous lesson. Direct students' attention to the "How Many Pets Do You Have?" graph. First in pairs, then as a class, discuss the following questions:

Q. **If all the students in our class brought all of their pets to school for a pet show, do you think we would have fewer than 50 pets, between 50 and 100 pets, or more than 100 pets? Why?** (Write "Fewer than 50 Pets," "Between 50 and 100 Pets," and "More than 100 Pets" where all can see.)

• • • •

• • • •

Mathematical Emphasis

Choosing a process for making calculations depends on the numbers themselves and how the results will be used.

Q. **What strategies** (mental computation, calculators, paper and pencil, or a combination of strategies) **might you use to determine the exact number of pets students in our class have? Why?**

Q. **What does each dot on the "How Many Pets Do You Have?" graph represent?** (Each dot represents a certain number of pets. For example, one dot in the "2" column indicates that one student owns two pets.)

Students need many opportunities to decide which computation method to use. In many cases an estimation is sufficient. When a more exact answer is needed, students' decision to use paper and pencil, a calculator, mental computation, or a combination of methods will depend on the numbers involved and the way the data are organized.

Explain that pairs will choose a strategy and then find the total number of pets. Facilitate a discussion about how students might work well together. Ask students to discuss the need for explaining their thinking and checking for understanding.

| **Notes** | **Teacher** | **Students** |

Notes

As you observe students working, ask yourself questions, such as:

Q. Do students choose a method of calculation that seems appropriate for the types and quantity of numbers?

Q. If students are using a calculator to compute, do they have a sense of the reasonableness of the sum computed on the calculator?

Also, observe how partners interact. Note positive interactions and any problems you might discuss when the class reflects on the lesson.

Teacher

Observe pairs working and, when appropriate, ask questions, such as:

Q. What strategy are you using? Why did you choose that strategy?

Q. How are you checking to make sure that you and your partner understand your work?

Q. How can you be sure your total number of pets is reasonable?

Students

In pairs, students determine the total number of pets students in the class have.

Mathematical Emphasis

Problems may have more than one solution and may be solved in a variety of ways.

Have several pairs share their strategies and results. Discuss and check for agreement on the part of the class. Ask students to explain why they agree or disagree. Ask questions, such as:

Q. How did you determine the total number of pets?

Q. Did any pair use a different strategy to determine the number of pets? How did you use that strategy?

•• ••

•• ••

Social Emphasis

Analyze the effect of behavior on others and on the group work.

Help students reflect on their work together by having pairs discuss with each other what they think went well today, what they think did not go well, and how that made them feel. Have pairs discuss something they would like to do differently the next time they work together. Ask if any pair would like to share with the class what they discussed.

If appropriate, share some of your observations of the positive interaction and any problems you noted as pairs worked.

Extensions

For Pairs That Finish Early

- Have pairs write about how they found the total number of pets students in the class have. Encourage students to write about their strategy in detail.

For the Next Day

- Have pairs consider the following:

    In a call to the Humane Society I learned that for every person born, five dogs are born. How many dogs are born for every two people? Three people? Four people? Ten people? What patterns do you notice? How many dogs were born all together for every student in our class?

    Ask pairs to write about how they solved this problem. Have the class discuss the solution and strategies pairs used.

Pets, Pets, Pets!

Students individually mark on a class graph the number of each kind of pet they have. Pairs write statements about the graph and analyze the data. This lesson may take more than one class period.

DAYS AHEAD
1

Mathematical Emphasis

In this lesson, students

- Collect, organize, and interpret data.
- Write statements summarizing data.

Students add to their understanding that

- Questions about our world can be asked, and data about those questions can be collected, organized, and analyzed.
- Numbers can be used to describe quantities.

Social Emphasis

In this lesson, students

- Explain their thinking.
- Listen to the thinking of others.
- Agree on statements to write.

Students continue to

- Develop group skills.
- Analyze the effect of behavior on others and on the group work.

Group Size: 2

Teacher Materials

- "How Many of Each of These Pets Do You Have?" graph (see Before the Lesson)
- Markers
- "Do You Have a Pet?" and "How Many Pets Do You Have?" graphs (from Lesson 2)
- Self-adhesive dots

Student Materials

Each student needs

- Paper and a pencil

Extension Materials

- Books about pets (see the Overview, p. 144)

Each pair needs

- Paper and a pencil

Each student needs

- Drawing paper
- Crayons or markers

- Make the following graph on a large sheet of paper.

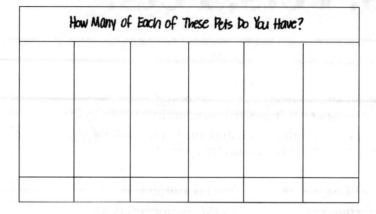

How Many of Each of These Pets Do You Have?					

- Have an activity available to engage pairs waiting to plot their data during the lesson (see Extensions For Pairs That Finish Early).

Notes	Teacher	Students
Post the "Do You Have a Pet?" and "How Many Pets Do You Have?" graphs (from Lesson 2).	First in pairs, then as a class, review the previous lesson by discussing questions, such as:	•• •• •• ••
	Q. What information were we able to learn from the data on the "Do You Have a Pet?" and "How Many Pets Do You Have?" graphs? What information couldn't we learn?	
Make sure that every pair has at least one student who owns a pet. If one student does not have a pet, ask the pair how they might include each other in the activity. For example, the student without pets might act as the recorder for the student with the pets.	Explain that today pairs will investigate how many of each kind of pet their classmates have, graph that information, and write statements summarizing the data. Ask each student to list the kinds of pets and the number of each kind of pet he or she has, then to share their lists with one another.	
	Observe pairs working and, when appropriate, ask question, such as:	•• In pairs, students
	Q. How are you helping each other with this activity?	**1.** Individually list the kinds of pets and the number of each kind of pet they have.
	Q. Why is it important to listen to your partner?	**2.** Share their lists with each other.

Notes	Teacher	Students

Notes

Post the "How Many of Each of These Pets Do You Have?" graph where all can see.

Alternatively, ask students to suggest how to organize the data on the graph and have students mark the graph using one of their suggestions. For example, students might suggest using one self-adhesive dot for every two pets, or having each student write the number of pets they have in the appropriate categories.

Teacher

Direct students' attention to the "How Many of Each of These Pets Do You Have?" graph. Ask students what kind of pets they have. As students state the different kinds of pets, list them along the bottom of the graph. Ask questions, such as:

Q. If you put one dot on the graph for each pet you have and you have three cats and one dog, how will you mark this graph?

Ask several students to model for the class how to mark the graph. Then have the rest of the students put a self-adhesive dot on the graph for each pet they have.

Students

•• ••

•• ••

Mathematical Emphasis

Questions about our world can be asked, and data about those questions can be collected, organized, and analyzed.

Students might suggest grouping and counting the data by groupings such as twos, fives, or tens. Choose one of the counting strategies and have students demonstrate how to count the data using that strategy.

Teacher

Refer to the "How Many of Each of These Pets Do You Have?" graph. First in pairs, and then as a class, discuss questions, such as:

Q. What do the data tell us?

Q. Where are the data clumped?

Q. How might we group the data to count them more easily?

Q. Look at the data on the graph. What statements can you make about our classmates' pets?

Write several of the pairs' statements where all can see. Discuss the statements made by pairs and check for agreement on the part of the class. Ask students to explain why they agree or disagree.

Have pairs write several summary statements about the data on the graph.

Students

•• ••

•• ••

Notes	Teacher	Students

Notes

Use the pairs' written statements to help you assess students' ability to interpret the data. Students will demonstrate different levels of sophistication when interpreting data. For example, some students might make the following statements:

- There are more dogs than cats.
- There are just as many hamsters as rabbits.

Other students might make the following statements:

- There are twice as many dogs as cats.
- About half of our pets are fish.

Teacher

Observe pairs as they write and, when appropriate, ask questions, such as:

Q. What are you and your partner doing that is helping you work together? Do you need to change anything? What might work better?

Q. How do you know your statements make sense?

Students

••

In pairs, students write summary statements about the data on the "How Many of Each of These Pets Do You Have?" graph.

Notes

You may wish to do this part of the lesson in a second class period.

Provide sufficient time for students to explore this question.

Teacher

Ask several pairs to share their statements. Discuss them and check for agreement on the part of the class. Ask students to explain why they agree or disagree. Encourage students to explain and justify their thinking, and have other students explain why they agree or disagree.

First in pairs, and then as a class, discuss the following questions:

Q. Are more than half or less than half of the pets in our class [cats]? How do you know? Did any pair use a different strategy to solve this problem? Explain.

Q. What information does this graph (point to the "How Many of Each of These Pets Do You Have?" graph) **tell us that is the same or different from the information on these two graphs** (point to the two graphs from Lesson 2)**? How do you know?**

Students

•• ••

•• ••

Notes	Teacher	Students

Social Emphasis
Analyze the effect of behavior on others and on the group work.

Help students reflect on the lesson by asking questions, such as:

Q. **What did you like about how you and your partner worked together? What problems did you have? Did your problems affect your work? If so, how?**

If students indicate that they had problems working together, ask them to discuss with their partner what they did that got in the way and what they could do differently the next time they work together. Ask if any pair would like to share with the class what they discussed.

•• ••

•• ••

Extensions

For Pairs That Finish Early

■ As students wait while others plot their data on the graph during the lesson, have them draw a picture of one of their pets or have them read a book about pets. You may want to display their pictures on a bulletin board.

For the Next Day

■ Have pairs choose one kind of pet listed on the "How Many of Each of These Pets Do You Have?" graph, research information about the pet, and write about how to care for it. Have students share the information with the class.

Pet Problems

Students write and solve problems using information from one of the graphs developed in the previous lessons.

Mathematical Emphasis

In this lesson, students

■ Write and solve problems.

Students add to their understanding that

■ Questions about our world can be asked, and data about those questions can be collected, organized, and analyzed.
■ Problems may have more than one solution and may be solved in a variety of ways.

Social Emphasis

In this lesson, students

■ Agree on problems to write.
■ Share the work.

Students continue to

■ Develop group skills.
■ Relate the values of fairness, caring, and responsibility to behavior.

Group Size: 2

Teacher Materials

■ "Do You Have a Pet?" and "How Many Pets Do You Have?" graphs (from Lesson 2)
■ "How Many of Each of These Pets Do You Have?" graph (from Lesson 4)

Student Materials

Each pair needs

■ Paper and a pencil
■ Access to a calculator

Extension Materials

■ Box to hold index cards

Each pair needs

■ 2 index cards
■ Access to a calculator

Notes	Teacher	Students

Students

•• ••

•• ••

Post the three graphs from Lessons 2 and 4.

A cooperative structure such as "Turn to Your Partner" (see p. xii) can provide opportunities for all students to become involved in the discussion.

Direct students' attention to the graphs from the previous lessons. Facilitate a class discussion about the graphs. Discuss questions, such as:

Q. How many of each kind of pet do the students in our class have?

Q. Which kind of pet do our classmates have more of than any other?

Write the following problems where all can see:

> **Our classmates have [12] dogs and [10] cats. How many dogs and cats in total do our classmates have?**

Note that this is an incomplete problem. It is intended to encourage discussion among students.

> **Our classmates have [5] rabbits, [4] hamsters, and [1] snake.**

Ask questions, such as:

Q. How might you solve these problems? Do they give you sufficient information? Explain.

Q. How might you change the second problem so that it makes sense?

Provide sufficient time for pairs to create and discuss possible problems.

Q. What is another problem you could solve using the information from the graphs?

Write several of the students' suggested problems where all can see.

If students do not have much experience writing problems, this activity might be difficult. Students need many opportunities to practice writing problems and to get feedback from other students about how they might write problems more clearly.

First in pairs, then as a class, discuss each problem and how it might be solved. Discuss whether the problems have all the information needed in order to solve them. Ask questions, such as:

Q. What information is included in the problems?

Q. Do all of the problems make sense? Which ones do not make sense? Why? How can we make these problems more clear

Explain that pairs will write problems using the information from the graphs. Pairs will solve the problems to be sure they make sense and can be solved.

Notes	Teacher	Students

Remind students that they should solve the problems they write.

Observe students and, when appropriate, ask questions, such as:

Q. How are you sharing the work? Is that fair?

Q. How are you making sure the problems make sense? How do you know if each problem has all the needed information?

Q. What strategies could be used to solve this problem? Can this problem be solved mentally? How?

••

In pairs, students write problems using the information from the graphs.

Have several pairs share a problem with the class. Explain that the class will give feedback on the problems. Ask students to discuss ways they can comment on and give feedback to other pairs in a caring and respectful way.

•• ••

•• ••

First in pairs, then as a class, discuss the problems and possible solutions. Ask questions, such as:

Q. Does this problem make sense? If not, how can it be made clearer?

Q. How did you solve this problem? Did anyone solve it in another way?

Q. Which problems were easy to solve mentally? Why?

Q. For which problems did you use a calculator? Why?

Q. How does it feel to share your problems with the class?

Social Emphasis
Relate the values of fairness, caring, and responsibility to behavior.

Help students reflect on the lesson by having students discuss with their partner how they think they have worked responsibly and how they could work more responsibly. Ask if any pair would like to share with the class what they discussed.

**For Pairs That
Finish Early**

- Have pairs choose two of the problems they wrote, edit them as needed, then copy them onto index cards with the answers on the back of the cards. Have them put the problems into a class Pet Problems Box.

**For the
Next Day**

- Have pairs copy two of their problems onto index cards, if they have not already done so. Put the problems into the class Pet Problems Box. Provide time for pairs to solve each other's problems.

Facts About Pets

Students measure themselves and compute informally to solve problems comparing their height to the height of a pony.

Mathematical Emphasis

In this lesson, students

- Use measurement to solve problems.
- Compute informally to solve problems.

Students add to their understanding that

- Operations can be carried out in a variety of ways.
- Problems may have more than one solution and may be solved in a variety of ways.
- Measurement is approximate. Objects can be measured by making direct comparisons.

Social Emphasis

In this lesson, students

- Help each other.
- Explain their thinking.
- Check for understanding.

Students continue to

- Develop group skills.
- Relate the values of fairness, caring, and responsibility to behavior.

Group Size: 2

Teacher Materials

- Transparency of "Facts About Pets" group record sheet

Student Materials

Each pair needs

- "Facts About Pets" group record sheet
- Yardstick or inch tape measure
- Access to a calculator
- Paper and a pencil

Extension Materials

- Pet Problems Box (from Lesson 5)

Each pair needs

- Drawing paper
- Crayons or markers

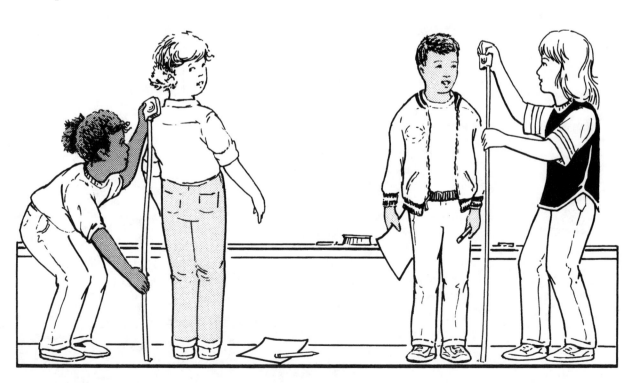

Introduce the lesson by facilitating a discussion about interesting facts students have learned about pets. Share and discuss the following facts:

These facts are taken from *The Kid's World Almanac of Animals and Pets* by Deborah G. Felder (New York: World Almanac, 1989).

- Some adult miniature dogs weigh only one pound.

- One Saint Bernard dog was recorded as weighing 310 pounds.

- The United States of America has a cat population of 56.2 million, the largest cat population in the world.

- The heaviest breed of cat is a Ragdoll. It can weigh up to 30 pounds.

Show the "Facts About Pets" transparency, read the directions, and explain that students will determine the height of a pony in inches and compare their own height to the height of a pony.

Facilitate a discussion about responsible ways to work.

Social Emphasis
Relate the values of fairness, caring, and responsibility to behavior.

Notes	Teacher	Students

Observe pairs and ask yourself questions, such as:

Q. Are the students able to compute 4×14? How? Do they use a calculator, paper and pencil, or mental computation? For example, some students might compute as follows:
$14 = 10 + 4$, and
$4 \times 10 = 40$, and
$4 \times 4 = 16$, and
$40 + 16 = 56$, so
a 14-hand pony is 56 inches high.

Q. When measuring each other, do students align the zero on the tape measure with the bottom of their feet?

Q. When measuring each other, how do students deal with fractional parts of an inch? For example, some students might say that they are about 49 inches tall, or a little more than 49 inches tall, or between 49 and 50 inches tall. Other students might say that they are close to $49\frac{1}{2}$ inches tall.

Observe how partners interact. Note positive interactions and any problems you might discuss when the class reflects on the lesson.

Observe pairs working and, when appropriate, ask questions, such as:

Q. How are you helping each other with this activity?

Q. How are you solving this problem? What other strategies might you use to solve this problem?

In pairs, students complete the "Facts About Pets" group record sheet.

Notes	Teacher	Students

Ask several pairs to share their results and their strategies for solving the problems on the "Facts About Pets" group record sheet. Discuss the solutions and check for agreement on the part of the class. Ask students to explain why they agree or disagree. Ask questions, such as:

Q. Are you or your partner taller than a 14-hand pony? How do you know?

Q. How did you record your heights? Why did you record your heights that way? Did any pair do it differently? How?

Q. Given what you know about the height of ponies, do you think I am taller than a 14-hand pony? Why?

Social Emphasis
Relate the values of fairness, caring, and responsibility to behavior.

Help students reflect on their work together by having pairs discuss with each other what they think went well and how they worked in responsible ways. Ask if any pair would like to share with the class what they discussed.

If appropriate, share some of your observations of the positive interactions and any problems you noted as pairs worked.

Extensions

For Pairs That Finish Early

- Have pairs choose a problem to solve from the class Pet Problems Box (see Lesson 5).

For the Next Day

- Have students show the approximate comparison of their height to a pony by having them draw a picture of themselves standing beside a pony.

Facts About Pets

A horse's height is measured in hands. A hand equals about 4 inches. Any small horse that is about 14 hands high or less is considered to be a pony. About how many inches high is a 14-hand pony? Record your work here.

How does your height in inches compare to the height of a 14-hand pony? How many hands high are you? Record your work here.

Information taken from *The Kids' World Almanac of Animals and Pets* by Deborah G. Felder (New York: World Almanac, 1989).

Pet Show

Students compute informally and use logical reasoning to solve problems. This lesson will take more than one class period.

Mathematical Emphasis

In this lesson, students

- Compute informally to solve problems.
- Use logical reasoning to solve problems.

Students add to their understanding that

- Operations can be carried out in a variety of ways.
- Problems may have more than one solution and may be solved in a variety of ways.
- Logical reasoning can be used to solve problems.

Social Emphasis

In this lesson, students

- Check for understanding.
- Agree to solutions.
- Make decisions.

Students continue to

- Develop group skills.
- Analyze the effect of behavior on others and on the group work.
- Take responsibility for learning and behavior.

Group Size: 2

Teacher Materials

- Transparency of "A Pet Show Graph"
- Transparency of "Pet Show" group record sheet

Student Materials

Each pair needs

- "A Pet Show Graph"
- "Pet Show" group record sheet
- Access to a calculator

Extension Materials

Each pair needs

- "A Pet Show Graph"
- "Pet Show: Extension" group record sheet
- Paper and a pencil
- Scissors

Introduce the lesson by explaining that you know a class that had a pet show. Students brought their pets to school, and the class made a graph to represent the number of pets at the show. Show the "A Pet Show Graph" transparency. Explain that each ✕ on the graph represents two pets. First in pairs, then as a class, discuss the following:

Q. How many of each kind of pet did students bring to the pet show?

Q. How did the class represent one pet on the graph? (A \ mark means one pet.)

Q. How did you count the data?

Explain that, in order to organize the show, the students in the class had to solve several problems. Show the "Pet Show" transparency and read the problems. Wonder aloud about the solutions to these problems. Ask pairs to choose three of the problems, solve them, and then write about how they solved one of the problems.

Social Emphasis
Analyze the effect of behavior on others and on the group work.

Facilitate a discussion about how students might work well together by asking questions, such as:

Q. How can you check each other's understanding as you solve the problems? Why is that important?

Q. Sometimes one person in a pair makes all the decisions. How do you think the other person in your pair feels when this happens?

Q. How can you be sure you and your partner are both involved in making decisions?

Notes	Teacher	Students

Mathematical Emphasis

Problems may have more than one solution and may be solved in a variety of ways.

Some of the problems may be a challenge for some students. Encourage students to persist, or suggest going to another problem and then returning to the one causing difficulty.

Observe pairs working and, when appropriate, ask questions, such as:

Q. **Which problems are you solving? Why did you choose these problems?**

Q. **How are you solving this problem? What other strategies might you use to solve the problem?**

Q. **How are you making sure you understand the problem and the strategy you and your partner are using to solve the problem?**

Q. **How are you making decisions? Do you both think this is fair? Why?**

●● In pairs, students

1. Choose three problems to solve on the "Pet Show" group record sheet.

2. Solve the problems, then write about how they solved one of the problems.

Students begin to clarify and solidify their ideas by explaining their own thinking and by listening to others. If students did not solve that particular problem, the class discussion gives them an opportunity to think about it.

Social Emphasis

Take responsibility for learning and behavior.

First in pairs, then as a class, discuss each of the problems. Ask questions, such as:

Q. **What did you need to know to solve this problem?**

Q. **How did you solve this problem? Do you agree or disagree with this pair's solution? Why?**

Q. **What other strategies did pairs use to solve this problem?**

Help students reflect on the lesson by asking questions such as:

Q. **Which problems were hard to solve? How did you feel when you solved them?**

Q. **What did you do to make sure you understood the problem? How did you make sure your partner understood the problem?**

Q. **In what ways did you take responsibility for your behavior? How might you work more responsibly?**

●● ●●

●● ●●

**For Pairs That
Finish Early**

■ Write the following problem where all can see and have pairs solve it
using the information on "A Pet Show Graph":

**One task students had at the pet show was to walk the dogs. If each
student walked only one dog, how many students were needed to
walk all the dogs at the same time? If each student could walk up to
three dogs at a time, how many students would be needed? How do
you know?**

**For the
Next Day**

■ Have pairs solve the problem on the"Pet Show: Extension" group
record sheet. (There is more than one solution to this problem.) As a
class, discuss pairs' solutions and strategies.

A Pet Show Graph

Number and Type of Pets at the Pet Show

Rat	Dog	Cat	Hamster	Bird	Fish	Gerbil	Guinea Pig	Rabbit	Snake	Mouse	Lizard
✕✕✕	✕✕✕✕✕	╲✕✕✕✕✕✕	╲✕	╲✕✕✕✕✕✕✕✕✕	✕✕✕✕✕✕✕✕✕✕✕✕✕✕✕✕✕✕✕✕✕✕✕	✕	✕	╲✕	✕✕✕	✕✕✕✕	✕

Each ✕ represents 2 pets.

Pet Show

Solve three of the following four problems. On a separate sheet of paper, write about how you solved one of the problems.

1. Use the information on "A Pet Show Graph" to solve this problem: The class bought water dishes for the dogs and cats. They decided to buy one dish for every two dogs and one dish for every three cats. How many dishes did they buy?

2. Use the information on "A Pet Show Graph" to solve this problem: The class decided to rent large cages for the cats. The store manager said that three cats would fit in one cage. The store was having a special discount on cat cages. How much money did the class spend renting the cages?

Special!
CAT CAGES
$2⁵⁰ each
Rent 4
and get the
5th one
FREE!

3. The class decided to put all the fish, birds, and cats on tables.

- Two tables were needed for the fish.
- Twice as many tables were needed for the birds as were needed for the fish.
- Four times as many tables were needed for the cats as were needed for the fish.

How many tables were needed all together?
Explain your thinking.

4. The students made a list of 150 people to invite to
   the pet show. They decided to divide the people into
   four groups so that everyone wouldn't come to the
   pet show at the same time.

   The smallest of the four groups had 25 people.
   How might the rest of the people be divided into
   the other three groups? What other ways are
   there?

Pet Show
Extension

The students needed to arrange the animal cages. They arranged six cages on a table by making three stacks of two cages. Follow these clues to decide how the cages might have been arranged. On the back of this sheet, draw a picture to show in which cages the animals were placed.

- The gerbil cage was stacked on top of the hamster cage.

- The rat cage was somewhere to the right of the mouse cage.

- The guinea pig cage was placed below the rat cage.

- The hamster cage was placed under the gerbil cage and somewhere to the right of the rabbit cage.

- The mouse cage was stacked above the rabbit cage.

You may want to cut out the boxes below and use them as you solve the problem.

gerbil	**guinea pig**	**rat**
hamster	**mice**	**rabbit**

Fantasy Pets

Pairs create a fantasy pet by combining three different kinds of pets, draw a picture of their fantasy pet, and list the pet's statistics and special abilities.

Transition Emphasis

In this lesson, students

- Describe attributes.
- Reflect on how they worked together.

Students add to their understanding that

- Numbers can be used to describe quantities.

Social Emphasis

In this lesson, students

- Share the work in a fair way.
- Listen to others.
- Agree on a fantasy pet.

Students continue to

- Develop group skills.
- Relate the values of fairness, caring, and responsibility to behavior.

Group Size: 2

Teacher Materials

- *The Whingdingdilly* (see Before the Lesson)
- Books about pets (see the Overview, p. 144)
- Fantasy pet picture (see Before the Lesson)

Student Materials

Each pair needs

- Crayons or markers
- Drawing paper
- Paper and a pencil

Extension Materials

Each pair needs

- Drawing paper
- Crayons and markers
- Paper and a pencil

- Obtain a copy of *The Whingdingdilly* by Bill Peet (Boston: Houghton Mifflin Company, Inc., 1970) or choose one or two books about a fantasy pet to read to the class.

- Create your own fantasy pet to share with students as you introduce the lesson. For example, you might draw a picture of a fantasy pet with a parrot's head, a Saint Bernard's body, and a rabbit's legs and tail. Look up some statistics about each animal and list your fantasy pet's statistics, such as:

  - **My fantasy pet weighs 180 pounds.**

  - **My fantasy pet eats less than 1 pound of seeds and fruit every day.**

  - **My fantasy pet can run 35 miles per hour.**

Notes

Social Emphasis
Relate the values of fairness, caring, and responsibility to behavior.

Have books about pets available for students to use to research specific statistics about their pets.

Teacher

Facilitate a class discussion about the previous lessons. Discuss questions, such as:

Q. **What mathematics have we been exploring?**

Q. **What have you learned about working responsibly?**

Introduce the lesson by reading *The Whingdingdilly* to the class. Facilitate a discussion about the story. First in pairs, then as a class, discuss questions, such as:

Q. **If you could have a fantasy pet, what pets would you put together to make your fantasy pet?**

Q. **What might your fantasy pet be able to do?**

Show your fantasy pet picture and discuss your pet's statistics. Explain that pairs will choose three kinds of pets and combine them to create a fantasy pet. State that pairs will create their own fantasy pet, draw a picture of it, and write a description of it.

As a class, brainstorm characteristics that describe pets, such as size, weight, special abilities and tricks, and foods they eat. List these characteristics where all can see.

Students

•• ••

•• ••

Notes	Teacher	Students

Social Emphasis
Develop group skills.

First in pairs, then as a class, ask students to discuss the importance of sharing the work in a fair way, listening to and respecting each other's ideas, and reaching agreement. Ask questions, such as:

Q. **What has helped you work well with a partner in the previous lessons?**

Q. **How can you be sure to share the work?**

Q. **How can you show your partner that you are listening to his or her ideas?**

•• ••

•• ••

As you observe pairs, ask yourself questions, such as:

Q. How do pairs work with each other? How do they treat each other?

Q. Do pairs listen to each other? Do they respect and build on each other's ideas?

Q. Do pairs come to agreement? How?

Q. What differences are there between how pairs worked together at the beginning of the unit and how they are working now?

Observe pairs working and, when appropriate, ask questions, such as:

Q. **What other special abilities might your fantasy pet have?**

Q. **How are you showing your partner you are listening?**

Q. **How are you making sure you agree?**

•• In pairs, students

1. Create a fantasy pet.

2. Draw a picture of themselves with their pet.

3. List statistics about their fantasy pet.

Have pairs share their fantasy-pet drawings and statistics with the class. Encourage students to ask each other questions.

Help students reflect on the lesson and how they worked together during the unit. Ask questions, such as:

Q. **What did you like about working with a partner?**

Q. **What problems did you have? How did you resolve them?**

•• ••

•• ••

Notes	Teacher	Students

Q. What did you learn about working cooperatively with a partner that might help other pairs work together?

•• ••

•• ••

If appropriate, share some of your observations of the differences between how pairs worked together at the beginning of the unit and how they work together now.

Give pairs an opportunity to thank each other and to share with each other what they liked about working together.

Extensions

For Pairs That Finish Early

■ Have pairs draw "photographs" of their fantasy pet. The "photographs" might show their fantasy pet at different ages or on special occasions. Have pairs contribute several "photographs" to a class photo album.

For the Next Day

■ Have pairs write a story about their fantasy pet.

Additional Reading

Mathematics Education

California State Department of Education. *Mathematics Framework for California Public Schools, Kindergarten Through Grade Twelve.* Sacramento, CA: California State Department of Education, 1992.

———. *Mathematics Model Curriculum Guide, Kindergarten Through Grade Eight.* Sacramento, CA: California State Department of Education, 1987.

Ginsberg, Herbert P. *The Development of Mathematical Thinking.* New York: Academic Press, 1983.

Kamii, Constance. *Number in Preschool and Kindergarten.* Washington, DC: National Association for the Education of Young Children (NAEYC), 1982.

———. *Young Children Reinvent Arithmetic.* New York: Teachers College Press, 1985.

———. *Young Children Continue to Reinvent Arithmetic,* 2nd Grade. New York: Teachers College Press, 1989.

Kamii, Constance, and Barbara A. Lewis. "Research into Practice: Constructive Learning and Teaching." *Arithmetic Teacher,* 38 (1990), pp. 34–35.

Labinowicz, Ed. *The Piaget Primer.* Reading, MA: Addison-Wesley Publishing Company, 1980.

———. *Learning from Children: New Beginnings for Teaching Numerical Thinking.* Menlo Park, CA: Addison-Wesley Publishing Company, 1985.

Mathematical Sciences Education Board. *Counting on You: Actions Supporting Mathematics Teaching Standards.* Washington, DC: National Academy Press, 1991.

———. *On the Shoulders of Giants.* National Research Council, Washington, DC: National Academy Press, 1990.

National Council of Teachers of Mathematics. *Measurement in School Mathematics.* 1976 Yearbook. Reston, VA: National Council of Teachers of Mathematics, 1976.

———. *Developing Computational Skills.* 1978 Yearbook. Reston, VA: National Council of Teachers of Mathematics, 1978.

———. *Applications in School Mathematics.* 1979 Yearbook. Reston, VA: National Council of Teachers of Mathematics, 1979.

———. *Teaching Statistics and Probability.* 1981 Yearbook. Reston, VA: National Council of Teachers of Mathematics, 1981.

———. *Estimation and Mental Computation.* 1986 Yearbook. Reston, VA: National Council of Teachers of Mathematics, 1986.

———. *Learning and Teaching Geometry, K Through 12.* 1987 Yearbook. Reston, VA: National Council of Teachers of Mathematics, 1987.

———. *The Ideas of Algebra, K Through 12.* 1988 Yearbook. Reston, VA: National Council of Teachers of Mathematics, 1988.

———. *Arithmetic Teacher,* 36 (1989). Special focus issue on number sense.

———. *Curriculum and Evaluation Standards for School Mathematics.* Reston, VA: National Council of Teachers of Mathematics, 1989.

———. *Curriculum and Evaluation Standards for School Mathematics Addenda Series, Grades K Through 6.* Reston, VA: National Council of Teachers of Mathematics, 1991.

———. *Curriculum and Evaluation Standards for School Mathematics Addenda Series, Grades 5 Through 8.* Reston, VA: National Council of Teachers of Mathematics, 1991.

———. *New Directions for Elementary School Mathematics.* 1989 Yearbook. Reston, VA: National Council of Teachers of Mathematics, 1989.

———. *Professional Standards for Teaching Mathematics.* Reston, VA: National Council of Teachers of Mathematics, 1991.

National Research Council. *Everybody Counts: A Report to the Nation on the Future of Mathematics Education.* Washington, DC: National Academy Press, 1989.

———. *Reshaping School Mathematics: A Philosophy and Framework for Curriculum.* Washington, DC: National Academy Press, 1990.

Sowder, Judith T., and Bonnie P. Schappelle, eds. *Establishing Foundations for Research on Number Sense and Related Topics: Report of a Conference.* San Diego, CA: Center for Research in Mathematics and Science Education, 1989.

Stenmark, Jean K. (ed). *Mathematics Assessment: Myths, Models, Good Questions, and Practical Suggestions.* Reston, VA: National Council of Teachers of Mathematics, 1991.

———. *Assessment Alternatives in Mathematics: An Overview of Assessment Techniques That Promote Learning.* Berkeley, CA: Lawrence Hall of Science, University of California, 1989.

Cooperative Learning and Moral Development

Artzt, Alice F., and Claire M. Newman. *How to Use Cooperative Learning in the Mathematics Class.* Reston, VA: National Council of Teachers of Mathematics, 1990.

Brandt, Ron (ed). *Cooperative Learning.* Educational Leadership, 1989–90, 47.

Brubacher, Mark, Ryder Payne, and Kemp Rickett. *Perspectives on Small Group Learning, Theory, and Practice.* New York: Rubicon Publishing Inc., 1990.

Cohen, Elizabeth G. *Designing Groupwork: Strategies for the Heterogenous Classroom.* New York, NY: Teachers College Press, 1986.

Davidson, Neil, ed. *Cooperative Learning in Mathematics: A Handbook for Teachers.* Menlo Park, CA: Addison-Wesley Publishing Co., 1990.

Johnson, David. W., et al. *Circles of Learning: Cooperation in the Classroom.* Alexandria, VA: Association for Supervision and Curriculum Development, 1986.

Kohlberg, Lawrence. "Moral Stages and Moralization: The Cognitive Developmental Approach." In *Moral Development and Behavior,* T. Lickona, ed. New York: Holt, Rinehart and Winston, 1976.

———. *The Psychology of Moral Development.* New York: Harper and Row, 1984.

Kohn, Alfie. "The ABC's of Caring." *Teacher,* 1 (1990), 52–58.

———. "Teaching Children to Care." *Phi Delta Kappan,* 72 (1991), pp. 496–506.

Lickona, Thomas. *Raising Good Children.* New York: Bantam Books, 1983.

Reid, Jo-Anne, Peter Forrestal, and Jonathan Cook. *Small Group Learning in the Classroom.* Scarborough, West Australia: Chalkface Press, 1989.

Schmuck, Richard A., and Patricia A. Schmuck. *Group Processes in the Classroom.* Dubuque, IA: Wm. C. Brown, Company, 1983.

Schniedewind, Nancy. *Cooperative Learning, Cooperative Lives.* Dubuque, IA: Wm. C. Brown, Company, 1983.

Sharan, Shlomo. *Cooperative Learning, Theory, and Research.* New York: Praeger, 1990.

Teacher Resource Books

Baker, Ann, and Johnny Baker. *Mathematics in Process.* Portsmouth, NH: Heinemann Educational Books, Inc., 1990.

———. *Maths in the Mind.* Portsmouth, NH: Heinemann Educational Books, Inc., 1991.

Barata-Lorton, Mary. *Mathematics Their Way.* Menlo Park, CA: Addison-Wesley Publishing Company, 1976.

Barnett, Carne. *Teaching Kids Math.* Englewood Cliffs, NJ: Prentice Hall, Inc., 1982.

Burns, Marilyn. *About Teaching Mathematics, A K Through 8 Resource.* White Plains, NY: Cuisenaire Company of America, 1992.

———. *A Collection of Math Lessons from Grades 3 Through 6.* White Plains, NY: Cuisenaire Company of America, 1987.

———. *Math by All Means, Multiplication: Grade 3.* White Plains, NY: Cuisenaire Company of America, 1991.

Burns, Marilyn and Cathy McLaughlin. *A Collection of Math Lessons from Grades 6 Through 8.* White Plains, NY: Cuisenaire Company of America, 1990.

Burns, Marilyn, and Bonnie Tank. *A Collection of Math Lessons from Grades 1 Through 3.* White Plains, NY: Cuisenaire Company of America, 1988.

Collis, Mark, and Joan Dalton. *Becoming Responsible Learners: Strategies for Positive Classroom Management.* Portsmouth, NH: Heinemann Educational Books, Inc., 1990

Dalton, Joan. *Adventures in Thinking: Creative Thinking and Cooperative Talk in Small Groups.* South Melbourne, Australia: Thomas Nelson Australia, 1990.

Elementary Grades Task Force. *It's Elementary!* Sacramento, CA: California Department of Education, 1992.

EQUALS. *Get It Together: Math Problems for Groups, Grades 4 Through 12.* Berkeley, CA: Lawrence Hall of Science, University of California, 1989.

EQUALS, Alice Kaseberg, Nancy Kreinberg, and Diane Downie. *Use EQUALS to Promote the Participation of Women in Mathematics.* Berkeley, CA: Regents of the University of California, 1980.

Freeman, Marji. *Creative Graphing.* New Rochelle, NY: Cuisenaire Company of America, 1986.

Gibbs, Jeanne, and Andre Allen. *Tribes: A Process for Peer Involvement.* Santa Rosa, CA: Center Source Publications, 1987.

Graves, Ted, and Nan Graves. *A Part to Play: Tips, Techniques and Tools for Learning Cooperatively.* Victoria, Australia: Latitude Publications, 1990.

Hill, Susan, and Ted Hill. *The Collaborative Classroom.* Portsmouth, NH: Heinemann Educational Books, Inc., 1990.

Hosie, Barbara. *Maths About Me.* Melbourne, Australia: Longman Cheshire Pty Limited, 1991.

Kagan, Spencer. *Cooperative Learning.* San Juan Capistrano, CA: Resources of Teachers, 1992.

Lappan, Glenda, William Fitzgerald, Elizabeth Phillips, Janet Shroyer, and Mary Jean Winter. *Middle Grades Mathematics Project.* Menlo Park, CA: Addison-Wesley Publishing Company, 1986. A series of five books for grades 6 through 9.

Meyer, Carol and Tom Salee. *Make It Simpler: A Practical Guide to Problem Solving.* Menlo Park, CA: Addison-Wesley Publishing Company, 1983.

Morman, Chuck, and Dee Dishon. *Our Classroom: We Can Learn Together.* Portage, MI: The Institute for Personal Power, 1983.

Rhodes, Jacqueline, and Margaret E. McCabe. *The Nurturing Classroom.* Willits, CA: ITA Publications, 1988.

Richardson, Kathy. *Developing Number Concepts Using Unifix Cubes.* Menlo Park, CA: Addison-Wesley Publishing Company, 1984.

Russell, Susan Jo, Rebecca Corwin, and Susan Friel. *Used Numbers: Real Data in the Classroom.* Palo Alto, CA: Dale Seymour Publications, 1990. A series of six books for grades K through 6.

Stenmark, Jean, K., Virginia Thompson and Ruth Cossey. *Family Math.* Berkeley, CA: Lawrence Hall of Science, University of California, 1986.

Whitin, David J., Heidi Mills, and Timothy O'Keefe. *Living and Learning Mathematics.* Portsmouth, NH: Heinemann Educational Books, Inc., 1990.

Wilson, Jeni, and Peter Egeberg. *Co-operative Challenges and Student Investigations.* South Melbourne, Australia: Thomas Nelson Australia, 1990.